desert country

desert country

by steve crouch

IMAGES OF AMERICA SERIES

DISTRIBUTED BY

CROWN PUBLISHERS, INC., NEW YORK

For Cookie
who was always there

Library of Congress Cataloging in Publication Data
Crouch, Steve.
    Desert country.

    (Images of America series)
    Includes index.
    1. Southwest, New—Description and travel—1951-
2. Baja California—Description and travel. 3. Deserts
—Southwest, New. 4. Deserts—Mexico—Baja California.
I. Title.
F787.C76   779′.9′9179   75-28929
ISBN 0-517-526395

FIRST EDITION

CONTENTS

OVERLEAF: *Saguaros in the rocky hills high above the Arizona desert stand like the columns of some Roman ruin half a world away.*

At sunrise the clear morning light turns granite
in the Mojave to gold; at sunset
the last long rays touch the red rock ranges
along the Colorado with flame.

Rains that fall in torrents upon the distant mountains send flash floods racing down the desert washes, sweeping away everything in their path.

Water from the storm evaporates under the dry winds
that follow, leaving no trace but the cracked mud patterns
in hollows of the desert floor.

OVERLEAF: Anywhere water is caught in a crevice,
desert plants put down roots and spring to life.

Prologue

MUSINGS OF A MINOR NATURALIST

The great Swedish naturalist, Carolus Linnaeus, who two centuries ago gave us a method for classifying all types of plants, once ranked all naturalists according to a descending scale of values. At the very bottom of his list, he placed that type of naturalist who is "much given to exclamations of wonder"—and not much else, according to Linnaeus.

I happily relegate myself to that category at the bottom of Linnaeus's heap—bumbling about my small corner of the earth, that section of the American West that includes the Pacific shore, High Sierra, and dry deserts. Within the compass of these lands lies such a variety of marvels that there is no end to the new and unexpected.

My first experience with the desert came a number of years ago when I left behind me the pine- and cypress-bordered bay of home and set out to visit a relative in southern Arizona. That seemed as good a justification as any—though truthfully it was simply a case of periodic wanderlust taken such hold as no longer to be denied.

The long route led southeastward through the velvety spring green of the California Coast Range and the valley of the San Joaquin; it climbed the slope of the Tehachapis until it

reached the basin at the summit where a smoking cement plant at Monolith sits in a dry meadow—a meadow that marks the beginning of the desert lying just over the ridge.

Beyond the ridge the promise implicit in the dry meadow became actuality. Grass cover succumbed to small, shrubby clumps of scattered bur sage; Joshua trees, their arms akimbo, replaced the familiar trees of the western slope. An immediate smell of dryness became pervasive. In the space of less than five miles, the transition from a moderate climate to one of severity could not fail to be apparent to anyone passing here, even to that preoccupied traveler who passes through life seldom seeing what lies on each side of his path.

The highway dropped down sharply on the eastern side of the Tehachapis to the gently sloping floor of the desert a thousand feet below. The road across the desert eastward from the town of Mojave, nestled at the base of the mountains, ran straight for miles across the basin—an expanse marked only by low vegetation, the Joshua trees being left behind on the higher slopes. In the distance, long stretches of gleaming white outlined the limits of one of this desert's dozen or more dry lakes. The road eventually rose to cross a small divide into another basin, lower than the first. The process went on interminably, each succeeding basin below the one before, down to those lower elevations where the Colorado River traces the border between Arizona and California.

Not far across the river appeared the vanguard of those stylized forms that symbolize the American desert, even to those who have never been closer to it than the banks of the Hudson River—the giant saguaros standing thirty and forty feet high, their arms semaphoring some arcane message that has never been deciphered.

In the desert washes there were trees that seemed like nothing more than puffs of smoke, so delicate were their branches and twigs. In other dry washes, with hidden stores of water beneath their sands, were palo verde trees heavy with yellow blossoms and humming with the insistent sound of uncounted honey bees. Whole hillsides above the washes were ablaze with massed beds of yellow blossoms that resembled small, delicate sunflowers—as indeed they were. There had been more than the normal rainfall in the winter just past, and the land was bursting with life hurrying to perpetuate itself before the onset of drought, which lay at most only short weeks away.

It took a long time to cross the Arizona desert that day. No great distances can be spanned when it becomes necessary to stop the car every few miles to see what strange cactus stands on the slope above the road, or what kind of fat lizard has scuttled into the rocks behind that clump of saguaros. An hour can be easily lost—or gained, depending upon the point of view—watching a curve-billed thrasher make her way in and out of a murderous cholla clump, where a nest is hidden and clamoring tiny voices announce the presence of new life within this bristling fortress. There are strange sounds to be investigated, sounds such as the shrill, birdlike cries of alarm that turn

out to be from a small ground squirrel perched on a dried branch, loudly objecting to this intrusion by a strange upright mammal poking and thrashing about—a dangerous behemoth at large in his territory.

So it happened that when the sun began its final plunge into the red haze above the mountains to the west, my destination still lay many miles away. It seemed both natural and desirable to drive off the road, through and around cholla and saguaro, until the highway was hidden from sight.

In those years my vehicle for exploratory missions like this was a medium-sized, sturdy station wagon of European manufacture. On its top was installed an ingenious boxlike arrangement that grudgingly opened, by means of a few tugs on nylon ropes and a well-articulated curse or two, to become a comfortable tent high in the air above any possible danger. In the desert twilight several curious birds perched briefly on nearby cactus plants to watch this establishment of temporary domicile. Then, having satisfied their curiosity, they flew off to attend to affairs of their own.

As darkness approached, the Coleman lantern began to cast a circle of bright light that illuminated the nearby cholla. Beyond in the diminishing brightness of the lamp's glow, other forms took on deceptive appearance, sometimes resembling cacti and sometimes, in my mind's eye, furtive figures encircling my campsite preparing to attack in force. For a time some small animal sat just outside the range of light, his eyes reflecting lamplight as he stared, shifting his position frequently for a better look. More than likely he was a friendly kit fox, drawn by the smell of cooking meat. The scraps laid out upon a bare rock remained untouched as long as the lamp was lit, but next morning only small grease marks were left to show where they had been.

Smoke trees' soft contours seem to ease the harsh face of the desert.

There is little to do in the desert wilderness after the sun has gone down, except to stare into the darkness and think of pleasant things or great imponderables—both equally important. Slight, cooling desert breezes stir the branches of the creosote bushes and add to a feeling of ineffable peace descending upon this particular patch of earth. Sleep comes quickly and completely.

Sometime close to midnight by imprecise reckoning, such a cascade of marvelous music came from above me that I was startled wide awake. A mockingbird had settled on the peak of the tent inches above my head and loosed a tor-rent of song upon the night that no instrument of man's devising has ever equaled.

The concert lasted all too short a time—it seemed at most a minute—and then began again, this time from a distance, as the performer made his way by moonlight to another perch. A final aria—then no more as he flew beyond earshot.

There and then in that bright, moonlit desert, which to some seems most forbidding yet to me most inviting, I found my place in Linnaeus's lowest stratum of naturalists—much given to exclamations of wonder and feeling little need of more.

THIS PLACE CALLED DESERT

Americans are particularly impressed by superlatives. They put great store by the man with the most assets, the ballplayer with the highest batting average, the young lady with the most generous dimensions. When the days of summer reach their longest, and thermometers across the land climb high and stay there, public interest turns to how high the mercury has soared and where it happened. No self-respecting television newscast or daily newspaper worthy of the name would fail to pinpoint these thermal excesses and hang a verbal blue ribbon on the town or city reporting the highest reading of the day.

So from June well into September, towns in the American Southwest claim records as, for weeks on end the temperature gauges of Thermal, Needles, Blythe, and Palm Springs in California, and Yuma, Buckeye, and Gila Bend in Arizona surpass those of the rest of the nation.

These are desert towns in the heart of the Mojave and Sonoran deserts. Even so, probably all these records would be regularly eclipsed if Death Valley were included in the daily report; it holds the signal honor of being the hottest place on earth during the summer months. Man, however, seems to attach importance only to those things directly related to himself; Death Valley, almost uninhabited during the hot season, is omitted in weather reports for the general public.

It is not by caprice of local weather conditions that these regions are consistently hotter than other places. The reason is that they lie directly beneath extensive masses of very dry, high-pressure air that collect here through dynamics of the earth's rotation and the resulting formation of worldwide wind patterns. These masses tend to remain in place; weathermen refer to them as semipermanent subtropical anticyclones—areas of stable air of little moisture that remain in fixed locations between latitudes of 20° to 30° on each side of the equator. They move north or south a few degrees with the changing seasonal tilt of the earth or when some violent storm disrupts them for a few days, after which they re-form in their accustomed place.

All the deserts of the world lie underneath these dry air masses. Look at a map of the world and follow the latitude of 20° south, as it cuts across the southern seas and continents. On the west coast of Chile and Peru lies the Atacama, a desert with the distinction of being the driest place on earth. Eastward beyond the Andes lies

Creosote bush and saguaro are hallmarks of the Sonoran desert.

the Patagonian Desert in Argentina and, across the Atlantic, the Namib and Kalahari in southern Africa. Still farther east lies the second largest of all deserts, the Australian, where most of a continent is desert save for an arable fringe on the outer edges.

In the northern hemisphere, there is even more desert, much more, simply because most of the earth's land mass lies north of the equator. The largest of all deserts, the Sahara, stretches across half of Africa along the 30th parallel, from the Atlantic to the Red Sea. Across that narrow finger of the Indian Ocean begins a belt of desert lands—the Arabian, Iranian, and Indian deserts, and then the burnt, dry lands of Turkestan, Takla Makan, and the Gobi.

Go on east across the Pacific and your traveling finger will come finally to the North American desert, an arid land reaching from the southern borders of British Columbia southward far down into the central plateau of Mexico, not far from Mexico City.

The northern half of this desert is the Great Basin, lying between the Sierra Nevada and Cascade Range on the west and the Wasatch and Sawtooth ranges on the east. The Chihuahuan Desert lies in southern New Mexico and western Texas, and extends south through the high plateaus of Central Mexico.

But the *real* deserts of North America, those that conjure images of furnace heat and vast, empty wastes, are the Mojave and the Sonoran, which lie in the southwesternmost quadrant of the North American desert. These are lands where often a year or more may go by without a drop of rain falling from the sparse clouds that pass overhead, lands where months may pass when thermometers climb above the hundred mark every day without fail. At one place in these deserts, the thermometer once soared to a searing 134.6°F.; at another place in the center of

the Mojave, 767 days once went by without a drop of rain reaching the ground. By any definition of desert, the Mojave and Sonoran stand in the forefront.

The Mojave is not a large desert compared with the others around it. It lies encircled on the north by mountains and higher elevations of the Great Basin, and on the west and south by the Sierra Nevada, San Gabriel, and San Bernardino mountains. Only on the southeast does it slope away gradually to lower elevations along the Colorado River. It has projections that reach out into the Great Basin—the Owens Valley in the lee of Mount Whitney, sizable portions of southern Nevada, a small corner of southwestern Utah, and a piece of northwestern Arizona lying close to the Colorado River. It is actually a transition zone between the high Great Basin and the low-lying Sonoran—a meeting place for more adventurous plant and animal life advancing south from the northern sagebrush desert and for hardier elements of the southern desert extending their range northward.

A moderately high desert for the most part, it falls off from four thousand feet in the north to less than two thousand feet along the mountains that signal its southern end. Along the Colorado it descends to an altitude only a few hundred feet above sea level. Death Valley, a basin of the Mojave hidden low in a fault depression between two mountain ranges, is an exception, much of its desolate area lying below sea level.

The Mojave is an extremely arid desert, beset by dry winds and shut off from the ocean's moderating influence; it gives little hint that not too long ago—as geologic time is reckoned—these bare basins were places of flowing rivers and deep lakes where plants and animals abounded.

At the end of the last Ice Age, barely 12,000 years ago, warmer lands untouched by glaciers spreading down from polar regions were deluged

Storm clouds pile up frequently over the ranges of the Mojave, but only occasionally does it rain.

with torrential rains—almost continual cloud-bursts, in effect. Lakes in the Mojave were fed by these abundant rains and by glacial melt from the Sierra Nevada and other nearby mountains. Water flowed into a series of lakes in the interior basins; as one filled up, it overflowed into the next lower basin, and that into the next until there was a string of interconnected pools, like pearls on a necklace, finally emptying into the lowest of all, thousand-foot-deep Lake Manly at the bottom of Death Valley.

There were trees and ferns and most of the other plants that grace a landscape when there is sufficient moisture. But in time, the climate changed, the rains dwindled to a gentle drizzle, and then it rained not at all. The more tender of the plants shriveled and died. The lakes shrank and dried up. Animals either migrated elsewhere or became extinct. Sometimes when an infrequent heavy rain fell, old lake beds became large bodies of water a few inches deep but dry winds quickly stole their moisture and left only white mineral salts leached from the mountains.

Long after, when European man came through these parts exploring for a trail from Mexico to remote Alta California, they called these great, white flats in the desert *playas*, the Spanish word for beach. Some of these playas are thousands of feet thick, storehouses of minerals deposited by the vanished waters. At Trona, on the playa now called Searles Dry Lake, work goes on night and day scooping up borax, magnesium, sodium, phosphates, and a dozen other minerals to make soap, water softeners, exotic rocket fuels, and a thousand products of modern man.

But most of the playas lie empty in the blazing sun, devoid of life. Indeed, the surface that looks so smooth from a distance is, in Death Valley, a rough, crystalline crust so salty that any living thing caught in it would be chemically embalmed within a matter of days.

Perhaps some day the rains will come again, but until then the flat playas will lie glistening but lifeless in the blistering sunlight, serving only as a speedway for overpowered automobiles and motorcycles or as a source of choking, blinding dust clouds when winds from the mountains rage across them.

The Mojave can support only the most tenacious of plants since rainfall averages less than five inches a year. Such measurements can be misleading, however. To sustain such an average often means that no rain will fall for a year or more and then two year's supply may fall in a few hours in some part of the desert, to run off quickly into the nearest dry lake leaving little moisture to nurture plants growing on the slopes of the basins. Since these plants cannot avoid drought, they must, perforce, endure it—adapting their growth habits both to avoid competition for what little subsurface water there is and altering physical structure to conserve whatever slight moisture may come their way.

Only along rare stream courses and beside desert seeps are there occasional willows and cottonwoods. In the higher desert their place is taken by xerophilic tree members of the lily family—tall, branching yuccas called Joshua trees, hallmarks of the Mojave. All else is low shrub and paltry grasses.

Yet despite its apparent hostility, there is an undeniable magnificence about the Mojave. Perhaps this is because, when the air is clear, the great immensities that are common to this desert reach out almost to infinity; mountain ranges rising up out of the desert floor a hundred miles away seem within close walking distance. Small wonder there are those who pass this way, pause a moment, and tarry for the rest of their lives.

South of the spreading basins of the Mojave, south of the Little San Bernardino Mountains, and astride the Colorado, where it leaves its gorge and moves slowly on its final course to the sea, lies the great Sonoran Desert, a land of many faces.

Like an enormous horseshoe, it encircles an arm of the Pacific—the Gulf of California, which the Mexicans originally named the Sea of Cortez. It stretches down the long, narrow peninsula of Baja California, covers most of western and southwestern Arizona, and the major part of the Mexican state of Sonora. Its northwestern limit reaches within a hundred miles of the great sprawl of Los Angeles, an arid land itself made habitable by waters appropriated from the Owens and Colorado rivers. At its southernmost limit, almost at the tip of Baja California, it touches the Tropic of Cancer, and blends with the tropical thorn forest in the southern part of Sonora.

Whereas the Mojave displays a majestic monotony, the topographic and climatic variations within the Sonoran create a place of great diversity. Desert plant life reaches its widest variety here; cactus grows tall and dominates the land. Yet existing within these limits is the driest of all American deserts, a land lying east of the Colorado at the head of the gulf. The Mexicans call it El Gran Desierto, an area so lacking in moisture that the only plant in its entire expanse is the toughest of all, the creosote bush.

This almost featureless plain may well be the harshest of all North American land. In a wet year, an inch of rain may fall—but then again it may not. The bastions of the San Pedro Mártir Range in Baja and the ranges lying between the desert and the sea in California effectively block all but the most powerful winter storms; the erratic summer storms from the Gulf of Mexico seldom reach this far.

Northwest of El Gran Desierto, stretching off for almost fifty miles, is a place of shifting sand—high dunes where little grows to halt the constant moving of grains of sand by desert winds. Travelers of a half-century ago made their way through these dunes on narrow wooden roads barely the width of an automobile. The remains of this old highway still lie in the sands, covered up by one wind, uncovered again by the next.

Beyond the dunes to the north is a sunken basin lying astride the San Andreas Fault, that great, shifting rift running two-thirds of the length of California from the gulf to where it disappears into the ocean north of San Francisco more than six hundred miles away. At some time long before history was recorded, long before man himself was present upon the earth, this basin sank below the level of the sea through block faulting and slippage common along California's widespread earthquake belts. It became an arm of the sea, a part of the gulf itself, until silt-bearing waters of the Colorado built a delta that shut off the basin and made its trapped waters an inland sea. In time the water began to evaporate under the assault of blazing sun and drying winds, and little came down from the mountains to replenish it. The sea shrank until it

became a small lake, then a salt marsh, and finally a great salt-encrusted playa lying more than two hundred feet below sea level.

Then once again the river changed its course, emptied into this great hollow, and filled it again; once more the delta formed a dam and left the waters to dry and the basin floor to be again a playa.

It stayed so until early in this century. Men saw the richness of the alluvial soils in the basin and cut a modest channel from the Colorado to bring water to spread upon newly planted fields there. The land blossomed; men sought to increase the land under plow and opened a second channel from the river. Water flowed gently, and the fields prospered. Then one day the river, swollen by floodwaters from mountains a thousand miles away, broke through its banks and began to pour into the canal, enlarging the breach in the river bank until it widened almost beyond repair. For a year and a half, the waters of the river emptied into the basin. When the breach was finally filled, a new sea covered the old lake bottom. Where once lay only a dry, white playa, the Salton Sea stands, growing more and more saline until its waters are now almost as salty as the ocean.

Both winter and summer rains fall in the uplands of the Sonoran Desert, that portion lying in the south central part of Arizona and the contiguous part of Sonora across the border; some parts are watered by as much as ten inches a year—a prodigious amount in a desert.

This is a land of saguaro forests and a hundred other kinds of cactus, which grow thickly upon the *bajadas*—great fans of detritus swept down from the mountains by erosion and deposited like huge, spreading skirts around their bases. The palo verde, mesquite, and ironwood cluster along arroyos, proclaiming hidden stores of moisture beneath the stream beds. After rainy spells, when the ground is well-watered, the earth is soon covered with small, ephemeral blossoms, annual flowers that turn the slopes into magnificent washes of color—often blooming twice within a year, responding to the torrential thunderstorms of summer and the gentler rains of winter, if they come. Spring comes upon these warmer deserts, not when the earth reaches its vernal equinox, but when water falls from the skies. Spring may be in February, or in June, or even in September. When it comes, there is no lovelier season on the face of the earth.

Across the Sea of Cortez lies a long, eight hundred mile finger of land pointing into the Pacific. Until a year or two ago, Baja California was as empty a wilderness as there was in the western hemisphere. The long dirt track that ran its length was more challenge than highway, forbidding to all but the most determined traveler. Now a ribbon of pavement stretches all the way from Tijuana to Cabo San Lucas; the *whoosh* of high-speed automobiles is a commonplace. But a hundred yards away from this lone artery, the wilderness remains. There are great silences—except for the sighing of wind through the cholla and the strange, rising chant of the cactus wren. There are mysteries here— lost missions and abandoned treasure, bones along the trail, hidden oases of palm and cottonwood. But few men pursue them; the land is too hostile.

All down the length of the peninsula, jagged mountains rise up to separate the marine terraces along the Pacific from precipitate cliffs edging the gulf. The whole land is still rising out of the sea in the east, tilting off toward the west. Few roads penetrate these mountains; most are burro trails at best. There are a few towns—San Felipe and Loreto and Mulege along the gulf shore, El Rosario and Guerrero Negro on the Pacific; San Ignacio is hidden in an unexpected forest of palms in a stream bed high on the central plateau. The only other signs of habitation here are small clusters of shacks—often just one or two surrounded by a scattering of corrals and outbuildings—located near waterholes with enough supply to support water-prodigal man. More of these settlements are now abandoned than occupied, the men who lived here dead or gone on to easier lands.

Some have named the sea between the peninsula and the mainland the Vermilion Sea; anyone who has stood on its shore and watched a stormy sunrise will know why. In truth, this sea is desert, too—lacking rainfall, seared by the sun, and swept by desiccating winds. Along its shores, the land lies arid and burnt. At its northern apex, rain seldom comes; the land is dune and lifeless bajada. The islands that are scattered down the length of the gulf are waterless and grim. Only when summer storm clouds gather is there lightning and thunder. Sometimes there is rain; often there is not.

The central half of the long peninsula is desert most unique—a biologic and ecologic island, isolated from the rest of the Sonoran Desert by deep water and high mountains. Behind these barriers are curious plants that grow only here in the Vizcaino Desert (named for the first Spaniard to touch its western edge). They grow nowhere else on earth and are strangely different from their kin on the mainland a hundred miles away.

Here grows the tall *cirio*, so named by the Mexicans because it resembled the slender candle they lit before the statue of the Virgin in their churches. The first American botanists to see it called it the boojum, a name applied to things most curious by Lewis Carroll. Looking like

Here and there in the Mojave, granite boulders lie scattered about the desert floor.

nothing so much as a pale carrot growing upside down, the boojum grows thickly on plateaus and slopes in the midsection of Baja. Where cold fogs from the Pacific float in and shroud the boojums on the western slope, they are small and covered with long strands of gray lichen that resemble Spanish moss of the American South. But on the slopes west of Bahía de Los Angeles, there are giants that grow seventy or more feet tall, reach-

ing for the sky with fingers of yellow flowers at their slender tips.

Sometimes the boojum grows straight, its single column standing like a long tapering spire against the sky, with small, twiggy branches only a few inches long that become stiff spines when their leaves fall. Sometimes it changes its mind when half-grown and forks into many trunks that stand apart like upthrust fingers. At other times, it reverses itself and bends down to meet the earth again, or sends its trunks out in great loops and whorls. A forest of boojums looks amazingly like a troupe of drunken ballet dancers. It is a member of the candlewood family and a relative of the ocotillo, which grows throughout the Sonoran Desert. But where the ocotillo has established residence over a range of a thousand miles or more, the boojum grows only in Central Baja, except for a small colony on the slopes of a few granitic hills on the coast of the mainland, slopes where seeds blown by some tropical chubasco found friendly soil.

Where grows the boojum grows the elephant tree, a strange tree that has no leaves most of the year and whose naked trunk looks all the world like a tapering elephant trunk. While it seldom grows more than fifteen feet high, its branches may spread over an area twice that in diameter. Like the cirio, the elephant tree loses its leaves in times of dryness and puts them out again when rain falls. As the tree grows, its thin bark peels in papery curls to reveal a blue-green inner bark beneath. Before going into dormancy, it bursts forth into a mass of flowers either pink or white—two colors that give the tree its Latin name, *Pachycormus discolor*, meaning thick stump of two colors. Frequently the tree is host to dodder, a parasite that grows like a tangled mass of orange hair, sometimes completely veiling the tree so that it resembles a freestanding, orange cocoon in the bright desert sunlight.

Far south on the Magdalena Desert, the section that marks the extremity of the Sonoran Desert, grows a strange cactus that some have called the creeping devil and others the caterpillar cactus. Its branches, instead of standing upright, are recumbent upon the ground. As new growth forms at the tip of each fiercely armed branch, the other end dies. Growing slowly—not more than an inch a year—each branch puts down roots and,

independent of its parent, becomes a new plant sending out its own new branches. These slowly expanding branches inexorably climb over any obstacle, including new branches they find in their path. In time they develop into a contorted, crisscrossed, and impenetrable colony with stems that may reach fifteen feet in length.

The whole of this long peninsula is a cactus jungle. Down its length grow no less than 110 species, sixty of which are endemic—they grow here and nowhere else. They range in size from the giant cardon, the largest of all cacti, to tiny rosettes, so small that only a close search will reveal them. Some of these cactus species grow elsewhere in the Sonoran Desert—cardon, organpipe, senita, and many of the cholla. But here they grow more exuberantly, their stems fatter and longer, their spines more ferocious, their flowers more gorgeous. Indeed, of all the deserts in the world, the variety and vigor of plant life on the deserts of central Baja exceed all others.

Living in this forest of cactus and trees most curious are animals that have also grown apart from their kin elsewhere, like the jackrabbits of one desert island whose color bears little resemblance to that of jackrabbits elsewhere. Over most of the world, jackrabbits have a coloration that blends with their surroundings, usually a pale buff that matches the dry grasses and sand-colored rocks of their habitat. Here on Isla Espíritu Santo, against a background of sand and dull red lava, thrives a breed of jet-black hares, whose ears sport a cinnamon-red trim. Their color provides little protection against either predators or the sun's punishing rays. No one has yet determined what unusual circumstances have made this jackrabbit so different from all the others of his kind.

On Santa Catalina Island, herpetologists have discovered *Crotalus catalinenses*, a rattlesnake that has no rattle. Instead, it has at the end of its tail a vestigial stump that makes no sound when the tail is vibrated. Whether this is a case of having lost the rattle because it is not needed—many of its predators are missing on this island—or because rattles have never developed, no one knows. But one walks carefully on this island.

A chuckawalla lizard inhabiting some of the gulf islands looks at first glance like chuckawallas elsewhere in the Sonoran Desert, but it has chosen an environment singularly lacking in fresh water—these islands have no springs or streams. When it rains, this lizard drinks deeply and stores so much water in small cavities within his body that he sloshes when he moves. When there is no fresh water, which is usually the case, he drinks salt water from the sea, and some marvelous mechanism within him is able to convert this salty drink into perfectly pure water. Man living in arid lands along the oceans would give much to know his secret.

There is a bat that is unique in that it prefers to skim over the sea, plucking small fish from the surface instead of foraging for insects like all other bats. There may well be other oddities of nature here, too. The peninsula is far from fully explored; except for the area near the long highway, the desert is accessible only to the determined.

The better-watered portions of the Sonoran Desert are thick with cactus. A few kinds of giant cactus are on both sides of the border. The senita—its bearded columns resembling a band of grizzled ancients, hence its Latin name, old man—and the organpipe intrude northward a few miles into Arizona; their entire range north of Mexico is encompassed within one national park set aside to protect the life of the desert.

The saguaro, thick upon the bajadas of Arizona, stands tall only a short distance into Mexico; before long, its place is taken by the larger and more thickly branched cardon. Scattered among these towering cacti are great thickets of cholla, stiletto-sharp spines gleaming in the sun, a united front against all intruders, save the birds that nest in its branches and the rats that use its joints to fortify their burrows.

There are barrel cacti, *bisnagas,* their spines closely woven about their fat, cylindrical shapes. Clumps of beaver tail cactus spread close to the earth, and small nipple cactus covered with tiny fishhooks often hide beneath larger plants.

These lands of Arizona and Sonora and those in the center of Baja California are the real cactus forests of the world. No place are there more in number or variety. And when spring and early summer come to these cactus jungles, blossoms cover each branch like orchids of the desert. No flowers are lovelier.

The mountains that rim the desert or stand in endless ranks about its floor are banded with stripes of red, black, brown, blue, and white—great strata hundreds of feet thick laid down beneath the waters of some ancient sea and then lifted and folded by tremendous pressures in the earth's crust. They offer a visual lesson in geology rivaled only by the walls of the Grand Canyon and cliffs in the canyonlands of Utah.

Other western ranges, like the Sierra Nevada, the Coast Ranges, and the Cascades, are crowned with the same stony crests, but lying as they do in the path of moisture-bearing clouds from the Pacific, their slopes are nearly covered with trees and shrubs, which break the harsh outlines and hide the face of the mountains.

Desert mountains are different. On their slopes little grows; indeed, there is precious little soil to furnish a welcome to any plant seeking a foothold, nothing to hold back forces of erosion that carve at these mountains when the hard but infrequent rains fall.

When rains do come, they fall in torrents but are quickly gone. The waters cascade down steep slopes, down sheer cliff faces in momentary cataracts, carving out gulches and washing down small pebbles and huge boulders. They roar down with their load of detritus, spreading their burden out at the base of the mountains in immense alluvial fans or bajadas, hundreds of feet thick and miles in length. These bajadas spread out unimpeded until they meet others. The entire desert floor, particularly in the Mojave, seems to be made up of these alluvial fans that stretch out forever—dry, rocky slopes covered with tough, xerophilic plants, creosote bush and bur sage, cholla and yucca.

The names of some mountains are a legacy of early Spanish explorers who came this way and mapped them—Cargo Muchacho and Pinto and Ajo, Cabeza Prieta and San Pedro Mártir, Picacho and Sierra Estrella. Indians gave names to others, which persist even until today—Baboquivari, Comobabi, Batomote, Harcuvar and Harquahala, and Sierra de Cocopah. When white men came seeking gold or surveying for railroads, the names they left behind celebrated experiences here or commemorated cherished lands far distant—Superstition and Growler, Mule and Music, Little Maria and Old Woman, New York and Providence and Bristol. Some of them are purely descriptive—White and Black, Calico and Chocolate. Often, they just memorialized themselves—Clark and Whipple and McCoy.

Seen from roads that wind through great, empty spaces, the mountains seem dry, harsh, and inhospitable—which in truth they are. Yet at the head of each bajada lies its source, a wash or canyon that cuts into the mountain and marks the course of whatever part-time streams exist there.

Beneath the dry sands of these watercourses lie hidden reserves of moisture; in the springtime, the washes are bright with the color of desert asters and verbenas and blazing stars. The air is heavy with the scent of palo verde and mesquite and ironwood; desert bees swarm at bright blossoms with endless buzzing. Life in the desert grows almost lush upon these washes. Plants thriving here produce seed that sustains small rodents living beneath stones beside the watercourses. These small animals in their turn provide the main food supply for predators—hawks, coyotes, kit foxes, snakes, and all the others that range these parched lands.

Most of the desert mountains are designated as "basin and range," a perfect description for the endless procession of low mountains separated by basins, which often have no outlet. In the Mojave, particularly, many valleys cradle a salt playa on their waterless floors.

But in the eastern quadrant of the Sonoran Desert, mountains rise eight or nine thousand feet high. In summer, air currents bearing moisture from the Gulf of Mexico pile great cumulus clouds atop these mountains, and sometimes thirty or more inches of rain a year will fall upon their slopes. Their bases are clothed with creosote bush and cholla, their middle elevations are thick with oak and sycamore and juniper, while their crests support Douglas fir, spruce, and pine. Winter snows lie deep on north slopes far above dry lands.

Near Tucson, mountain masses circle the city—Baboquivari to the southwest, Santa Catalina to the north; southeastward are the Huachucas and Santa Ritas. Birds from high, cool mountains far north live in evergreen forests on these summits. At the foot of the mountains, cactus wrens and roadrunners and curve-billed thrashers, common to all the desert, build their nests and spend their days. But on the middle

Lenticular clouds often course over the mountains of the northern Mojave, sure signs of powerful updrafts.

slopes are exotic birds from Mexico and Central America, who come this far and no farther to raise their young during the months of summer. There are coppery-tailed trogons from as far away as Chiapas; bridled titmice, busy birds flitting through trees in gossiping bands; painted redstarts, yellow-eyed juncos, and a half-dozen kinds of hummingbirds. High above the slopes, zone-tailed hawks ride the updrafts.

These mountains are oases—moist refuges where birds and plants and animals carry on their lives as if there were no desert surrounding them. Trees and shrubs grow thick and tall, and in rainy seasons, the sound of falling water fills the air. Coatimundis, comic Mexican relatives of raccoons are at home here; ocelot sometimes pace among the trees in remoter parts of the range; jaguars have been here within recent memory.

Far west are other oases where blue palms grow at the base of the San Pedro Mártir Range in Baja California, and fan palms grow thick in canyons at the base of the San Jacinto and Santa Rosa ranges beyond the Salton Sea. Long lines of palms mark the passage of the San Andreas Fault where it has disturbed the flow of underground water and forced it upward. For the palm is not like those desert plants that stand their ground in the driest of times and patiently wait for rain. Palm trees must have water always, and in plenty; they congregate about permanent springs and seeps and upwellings that never run dry. They are seldom found in the central desert where water is scarce; instead, they skirt the western edge of the desert along the eastern face of the mountains. In Arizona, only one remote cleft high in a canyon of the Kofa Mountains near the Colorado River supports a stubborn stand of palms. How they got there is a mystery; perhaps they are all that remains in Arizona of a species that once flourished here when the land was more moist than now.

There are other oases, hidden, unfrequented by man but known to every bird and animal that lives here. These are damp spots where water hides below the ground. Clever animals, wise in desert ways, dig and find enough water to sustain themselves. There are catch basins in solid rock—*tinajas*, the Mexicans call them—which hold enough water from rains to last a whole year and furnish it to every being that walks, crawls, or flies for a radius of twenty miles around. Under ledges are drips that may yield only a spoonful or so of water a day and yet mean the difference between life and death to some thirsty creature who depends upon them.

Man has preempted the more beautiful oases; in most cases, his advent has not been particularly beneficial. He has trampled the vegetation, filled the springs with litter, and has often stolen the water, forcing other inhabitants to withdraw to a more Spartan environment. Even the desert bighorn was driven from water and hunted to the edge of destruction, yet, like other species, it hangs on—a testament to the toughness of some of these desert breeds.

These oases in miniature, hidden in mountains scattered about the Mojave and Sonoran deserts, are the last chance for embattled creatures of aridity. They will probably survive here, simply because the waters are not generous enough to tempt man.

There are roads upon the face of the desert. Some mark ancient paths from one waterhole to another. Some were traced three hundred or more years ago, when Spanish columns first came this way searching for the riches of Cíbola, and priests followed, searching for souls to save along the Magdalena and Altar, the Gila and Colorado. Some of their marks still exist; the desert is slow to cover signs of man's passage. Other roads—racecourses of asphalt and concrete—no longer seek out the waterways but run straight across the deserts for miles. To most who pass this way, at speeds so fast that the roadside becomes no more than a blur, both the Mojave and Sonoran deserts seem unpleasantly forbidding, a land to be traversed as quickly as possible or shunned completely if there are other roads to take.

This dislike of the desert is nothing more than a primeval fear of an alien and intractable environment, a foreign land, a threat to one's well-being. Yet all around are a multitude of living things that consider this seeming waste of sand and creosote bush and spiny cactus a world ordered precisely as it should be—a perfectly adequate place in which to be born, to live, and to die. Man's vision is often of meaner proportions.

ARID GARDEN

Joshua trees, huge members of the lily family, stand in scattered groves in the high California desert.

Towering high above the omnipresent cholla, its arms reaching for the sky, the saguaro is a symbol of the Sonoran desert.

Along the border and far south into Mexico, the hoary senita
grows in thick clumps; its branches spread from its base whereas
the saguaro's branch out halfway up the trunk.

*Long leaves of yucca and short spines of cactus
play variations on the same thorny theme.*

HOME IS WHERE YOU MAKE IT

John Steinbeck once accompanied his friend Ed Ricketts on a voyage to the Sea of Cortez to collect marine life in the shallows along the shores of the gulf. During the course of the expedition, he learned a great deal about the life processes of the organisms they collected. In writing about them he observed that survival is the first commandment for all living things. All else is secondary—reproduction and any of the other functions attendant to the perpetuation of the species follow after the certainty of individual survival; all the tricks and mechanisms are aimed at that one end: to stay alive.

This is as true for the plants of the desert as for those marine slugs, sea cucumbers, and nudibranchs that Steinbeck and Ricketts concerned themselves with. Within an arid habitat, plants have three tasks: to get water when they can, to hold on to it after they get it, and to exist without it most of the time.

It would seem to most casual observers that plants in the desert must struggle against great odds to exist at all. Still, when everything is right, they function as do plants anywhere; they burst out in green foliage, they flower, produce seed and perpetuate the species. One would think that a more generous climate would make their task much easier. Yet when they are moved to a milder habitat they die or, at best, they do poorly. The harshness of the desert seems insurmountable only to those that are unequipped to cope with it.

Look closely at the desert; see how plants stand apart. On the driest deserts, there is wide spacing between each creosote bush, each bur sage. Even grass grows only in clumps or hummocks, taking care that roots do not compete for water with a nearby clump. Desert plants are, for the most part, dependent upon shallow root systems, spread wide to catch rain that may penetrate only an inch into the soil. There can be no appreciable competition between plants—there is not sufficient moisture to sustain two root systems occupying the same space.

There are members of the cactus family, not of the desert, that are as leaved as any ordinary plant. Cacti of the desert have long since abandoned leaves, those appendages normally involved in photosynthesis, the conversion of sunlight into sugar during which moisture is lost by transpiration through minute openings in the leaves.

To reduce this loss, cacti have shed their leaves, and photosynthesis is carried on by the green stem of the plant itself. Its spines are the vestigial remnants of those long-gone leaves. On some varieties, spines grow so thickly they serve to shade the plant from the sun.

The accordion-pleated saguaro is able to expand or contract its bulk according to the moisture hoarded in its pulpy interior. When a year or more goes by without rain, the pleats grow deeper and deeper, the trunk looking ever more shriveled. Yet let one reasonable rain soak the ground around it, and its roots will suck up two or three tons of water. Within days it will expand and become fat and flourishing.

Fully branched saguaro may weigh eight or nine tons; most of this is water. It needs much and has developed special techniques to get it. When rain falls, the saguaro within hours develops tiny, hairlike 'rain roots' to assist in harvesting every available ounce. When the ground is dry, the rootlets disintegrate and only the larger roots are left to anchor the saguaro in the earth.

This lack of leaves is not particularly unusual; there are many instances of it in the desert. In milder climates, plants drop their leaves at the onset of cold; in the desert, the onset of drought is the signal for leaves to fall. Ocotillos send long branches up from a central root crown. Most of the year, these limbs are bare. Within two or three days after a rain, their branches are thickly covered with dark green leaves. When the earth has dried, the leaves fall and once again the ocotillo stands naked against the harsh land.

Among a host of leguminous plants of the desert, palo verdes from a distance always seem to be in leaf. Yet close examination shows only tiny, green twigs and branchlets—no sign of leaves. Only after rains fall do these trees break out in leafy bud, to flower and then retreat into dor-

mancy again with the coming of drought. But dormancy is never complete; there is green chlorophyll in the bark, branches, and twigs of the palo verde to continue at a reduced rate photosynthesis within the plant even in the driest of times.

There are many members of the pea family numbered among the desert plants that stand and endure the worst this climate has to offer—palo verde, mesquite, senna, acacia, fairy duster, indigo bush, smoke tree, ironwood. After rain comes and the sands within the washes hold stores of water that bathe their roots, they break forth in such a frenzy of bloom that the air for miles is heavy with their pefume.

Probably the toughest of plants, the creosote bush is the most widespread of all in warmer deserts of the New World. It grows farthest north in that indefinite zone where the Mojave meets the Great Basin desert. It grows in the saguaro desert of Arizona and Sonora, on the sterile lands around the Salton Sea, among the boojums of Baja California. It endures the worst the desert can offer in the sub-sea-level sink of Death Valley, and it climbs 9,000 feet high on the altiplano in Zacatecas far south in Mexico. The same plant grows in arid lands in Texas and on the deserts below the equator in Chile and Argentina. No one knows whether it spread south from Arizona to Argentina or worked its way north. But it is a sure mark of the desert wherever it is encountered.

It is not a tall, tree-like shrub; its many well-spaced branches usually rise to a height of only four or five feet. On these branches are small leaves just a quarter-inch or so in length. Each bush, in places where drought is frequent, stands well apart from its fellows so that roots will not compete with each other for the little moisture available. This, with its small leaves and well-spaced branches, makes the plant seem airy and rather frail and unsubstantial. Nothing could be farther from the fact.

This tough creosote bush has adapted to the desert better than any other plant that grows there. Where Joshua tree, saguaro, and cholla grow, there the creosote bush flourishes; when barren soil stops the others, the creosote bush marches on. It is everywhere on these warm deserts, except upon the saline playas that are too poisonous to support any plant.

Its leaves are covered with a waxy resin that prevents excessive loss of moisture; crushed between the fingers, it leaves a sticky residue like freshly applied glue. When drought comes, the bright green leaves drop, leaving yellowish ones to carry on the reduced functions of the plant. Let drought continue and grow severe, these leaves will fall and only brown, dead-looking ones will remain upon the branches. At those times, practically all growth stops; the creosote bush almost ceases to be a viable entity until rains fall. Then leaves break out green again, the plant is covered with lovely yellow blossoms, and the creosote bush seems none the worse for its experience.

Nothing much feeds upon this plant, except an occasional rabbit that may sometimes nibble in passing. Only the camel, introduced here by Americans a century and a quarter ago, found the creosote bush to its liking. The camels have been gone for seventy-five years. The creosote bush seems likely to remain as long as the land is arid.

These perennials—creosote bush and bur sage, mesquite and palo verde, boojum and saguaro— are drought resisters, condemned to stand fast in the middle of great aridity. There are drought evaders that grow here, also. These drought evaders are annuals that sprout, grow, flower, and die in the short time that desert sands hold water after summer or winter rains. The rest of the time, ten months or more of every year, they exist only as seed hidden beneath a thin scarf of sand or blown about by desert winds. No matter, they are beyond any damage that heat and drought can inflict. They wait until conditions are exactly right before they come to life again.

These drought evaders are the plants that in wet years cover the floor of the desert with a great carpet of blossoms—poppies, phacelias, verbenas, primroses, and a dozen other brilliant kinds of bloom. Sandy wastes disappear under a blanket of brightness. Nowhere else does such a riotous abandon of color occur as among the slopes and dunes of the California desert.

In some marvelous way, these seeds have developed mechanisms that work to restrain germination until a series of conditions have been precisely met. Seeds of spring annuals only germinate when watered by cool rains during times of lower temperatures; summer annuals must have warm rain and high temperatures. Both kinds refuse to bestir themselves if there has been insufficient rain—as if they knew how much was required to see them through their short life. Only part of the seeds of some plants will germinate; the rest are held back in case of failure of the first crop to provide a reserve for later success.

One scientist has put it very well in commenting on the particularity that desert seeds exhibit in germinating or not. This insistence on optimum conditions before coming to life, the good savant refers to as "birth control." Botanists have theorized in dry technical terms about what causes the seeds to do as they do. Probably they are right, but desert lovers look upon it as a kind of magic sufficient unto itself.

Plants of the desert thrive here because they have made a structural adjustment to cope with their environment. They cannot go elsewhere, so they adapt themselves through mechanical changes or modification of organic function to exist within their surroundings. Some desert animals do the same. In small salty pools of the desert, there are fairy shrimp and pupfish descended from ancestors that lived here thousands of years ago when the land had many rivers and lakes. Because most waters where they live are intensely saline, these creatures have developed tolerance for concentrations of salt sufficient to kill ocean fish.

There are other examples of biological adaptation, but for the most part animals of saguaro, creosote bush, and cholla biomes meet the desert head-on through behavioral adjustments. The most formidable hazard they face is heat; to avoid it most animals here are either nocturnal or active mainly at dawn and dusk. But birds and lizards, which live on insects abroad in the daytime, must come out in bright sunshine to find food to sustain themselves. Birds confine their activities during the very hottest months to the hours near dawn and sunset. While the sun is high, they seek shade to survive, panting and dissipating body heat through the lightly feathered undersides of their spread wings.

Probably no animal has learned more adroitly to live well in the driest parts of the desert than the kangaroo rat—a small creature common throughout the desert, particularly along the edge of dunes or other sandy wastes, but seldom seen except at the flickering limits of a campfire or as a small flash of movement when the moon is full and bright. The kangaroo rat does easily what none of the larger animals can do: he is able to live entirely without water during his whole life. Further, he will not touch water in his natural habitat. His only foods are seeds and air-dry grasses, carbohydrates containing no water. Part of the oxygen he breathes combines with hydrogen in the food he eats to produce water within the body. Since a gram of starch within the rat's

body will yield approximately six-tenths of a gram of water by oxidation, considering the amount of seeds and dry grasses this small animal consumes during his life-span, he is not likely to lack for water, provided he conserves it properly.

Conserve water he does and very well. He cannot cool himself by water loss as man does by sweating or a dog by panting. Extremely small animals have such tiny body masses, which gain heat so quickly, that to cool themselves the expenditure of moisture on an extremely hot day would result in the loss of enough body weight to kill them within an hour. So the kangaroo rat does what he must in the way that is most practical for him—when the sun is abroad, he stays fast asleep in his burrow beneath the sand, where the temperature rarely rises above 85°. He is safe there from peril, except for an occasional rattlesnake that may join him to escape the heat and find a dinner, or some roaring dune buggy that tears the sands apart and demolishes his shelter.

The kangaroo rat goes even farther—his nasal passages are so constructed that they are cooler than the rest of his body. As his exhaled breath passes through, it is cooled and some of its moisture condensed and retained there. And when he retires to his burrow, he plugs the entrance with sand; his exhalations are trapped and the moisture breathed in again. He has an enormous kidney in relation to the rest of him, a kidney that removes practically all water from his feces, concentrating urea in his urine to such an extent that he excretes little more than dry pellets.

A marvelous machine for conserving moisture, this kangaroo rat—and like his kin, he reproduces generously when conditions are right. Thus he becomes a dietary staple for carnivores prowling the night in search of food—sidewinder, kit fox, badger, coyote, owl. Without rodents these carnivores could not exist here.

On warm spring days in the desert, one animal

is often abroad that seems most out of place in such waterless surroundings—the desert tortoise. He wears the same shell his ancestors have been carrying about for almost 200 million years—proof enough that nature seldom tampers with a successful experiment. He drinks deeply when he can and retains this water within his body against time of need. When the temperature soars, he burrows into the ground and awaits the cool of the evening. When he is abroad, his armor protects him from most predators, except the largest carnivores and man. Otherwise he roams the desert with great imperturbability—gnawing at leaves with toothless gums and observing the world through weary eyes.

In cooler seasons, carnivores may be abroad in daytimes hours as well as at night but on summer days, they seek out sheltered places to escape heat and conserve body moisture. Like all animals, they have limits to body temperatures that must not be exceeded, lest they die. So they come out only when the sun has dropped to the western horizon, congregating around small waterholes to replenish their water supply and to await whatever prey may come their way.

Mule deer and peccary come here to drink. Bobcats and an occasional mountain lion stalk them. Rarely a jaguar from the Sonoran mountains may wander into the edges of the southern desert, but both American and Mexican have almost eliminated him from this part of his range. Spotted and hooded skunks have the right-of-way because of certain built-in advantages they possess.

So the night is alive with living things that spend their waking hours in a relentless search for food. Mice gather seeds and dry grasses; packrats gather great piles of prickly pear and cholla joints to lay upon their mound-like dens. The coyote's cousin, the gray fox, sometimes puts in an appearance, as well as the animal scientists have given a Latin name *Bassariscus astutus* ("crafty, cunning little fox"). Scientists are seldom so inaccurate; the ring-tailed cat is neither cat nor fox, but a southern relative of the raccoon. More tail than body, it dines on mice, insects, cactus pads, and an occasional bird.

Bats and birds fly above or perch atop saguaro and yucca to search for prey in the air or on the desert floor. Snakes abound—lyre snakes, racers, leaf-nosed snakes, rattlers, and the timid but deadly Sonoran coral snakes. Scorpions come out from beneath fallen cactus branches seeking insects to seize and devour. Because scorpions and venomous serpents are primarily night crawlers, man seldom roams the desert at night.

Where animal life is most plentiful—on the upland slopes of the Sonoran Desert—there stands the great boardinghouse of the desert, the giant saguaro. When it is in its infancy, rodents devour it as a delicacy. Should it survive to grow tall, white-winged doves summering here from southern Mexico drink deeply of the nectar of its blossoms. When its fruit is ripe, Papago Indians use tall poles to knock them loose for food. Birds and insects eat what is left.

Gila woodpeckers carve holes high in the giant saguaro to raise their young; gilded flickers chisel theirs farther down. Elf owls and sparrow hawks use the same holes; thrashers, flycatchers, warblers, martins, bluebirds, and the ubiquitous English sparrow are tenants, too. Bats live in saguaro holes and packrats, fieldmice, spiders, mosquitoes, wasps, bees, and flies. Crows and hawks build massive nests of sticks and twigs among its branches. The saguaro has as mixed a clientele as any apartment house in the world.

It will serve its host function well for perhaps

two centuries until at last it tires, grows weak, and topples in some heavy wind. Even then it becomes a banquet table for a myriad of insects and animals that gnaw at its carcass until only the hard, woody ribs of its skeleton are left. In time, even these disappear.

It has been pointed out that the kangaroo rat makes eminent sense as a denizen of the desert. He makes efficient use of foods that grow around him; none surpasses him as a conserver of water. He can take the desert at its most demanding and live very comfortably in it. Man seems ridiculous in comparison. Almost without exception he tries to exist in the desert by making it as little like the desert as he can. He pumps the rivers and underground pools dry to irrigate his fields, water his lawns and golf courses, and refrigerate his habitations. He manages to expend water as prodigally as if there were an infinite supply.

Man has an overwhelming need to dominate—other people, other nations, the environment he occupies, everything with which he comes in contact. In the desert he has no less tendency to dominate and change. It is axiomatic that the dominant seldom share the fate of the helpless; instead, they determine it. Man may yet push this land and its denizens to the edge of disaster.

Yet by a curious paradox, this same drift may possibly save it. For if man exhausts the supplies of water that sustain him here—the ever more inadequate water from the rivers crossing the land, and the fossil water that lies deep beneath the ground—he must abandon the desert. Then those living things that were here before him— cactus, palo verde and mesquite, creosote bush and yucca, kangaroo rat and snakes, scorpions and birds—can go on about their business of making do with whatever water comes their way from infrequent rains, just as they did for thousands of years before man ever set foot here.

The road from Wildrose to Stovepipe Wells went straight for miles through the bowl-shaped plateau in the Panamint range. On each side plants common to high deserts stretched away in gray-green clumps up the slopes to the distant ridges on the east and west.

In the distance small herds of wild burros, descendants of those loosed a hundred years ago by gold seekers in these hills, moved placidly about seeking forage, their heads raised and ears cocked forward every now and then to scout the terrain for danger.

A rough-legged hawk, the pinions at the end of his wings spread like outstretched fingers, rode the air currents. Then suddenly circling twice in tight spirals, he plunged downward and disappeared into the brush. Seconds later, he rose on flapping wings and flew away—his luckless prey, a ground squirrel, hanging from his talons.

Black-throated sparrows, busy at domestic tasks in this nesting season, flew about picking at twigs and scraps, bearing them away to private construction sites in the branches of the taller plants. Frequently they paused to pour forth cascades of song, whether to announce their territorial claims or merely to herald the advent of spring only they could know.

On the ground, so camouflaged that he seemed when motionless to be part of the stony soil, a hungry Cro-talus confluensus moved slowly along, first this way and then that, pausing frequently to sense what lay ahead, his black tongue flicking out nervously and continually. Small sensitive depressions below his un-blinking eyes were alert to any minute change in temperature in the space before him, changes which could indicate the presence of small, warm-blooded animals to provide him his next meal, long overdue after a time of poor hunting. Or perhaps instead of food, he sought a female of his species to consummate the urges besetting him in the warming land.

His tan skin was faintly marked with a vague, diamond-shaped pattern; his only peculiarity of color was the lovely turquoise patch at his throat. As he moved about, he held his tail proudly erect so that the horny, rattling buttons at the tip would be ready to sound a warning to trespassers and interlopers. In the patch of land that was the limit of his experience, he was the undisputed king of all its inhabitants that moved upon the ground.

As the afternoon wore on to its midpoint, he moved carefully about his domain, around stones and small obstacles in his circuitous path. Not once did he sense even a trace of prey; not once did he come upon a female of his kind.

At length he made his way to the west until he came upon a long, unnatural depression. Beyond this barrier he had never ventured before, but since his hunger was gnawing at him fiercely, he made his way cautiously down into the ditch and then labored up the other side, a task made difficult by the loose soil that made him slide back often. Eventually he reached the top and paused to consider before venturing forth upon the twenty-four feet of smooth and slippery black asphalt that confronted him.

At this moment, miles to the north, an enemy approached, roaring up along the road from the great desert valley below. He was clad from neck to toe in gleaming black leather; his head was enclosed in a round, gleaming helmet with a transparent visor to bar the wind from his eyes. Behind him, dressed identically, clung his mate, her arms around his waist as they came speeding up the wash leaving a wake of almost deafening sound beating against the walls. They burst out of the wash onto the plateau with a great surge of power, and the cycle leaped ahead on the black ribbon of flat road.

Crotalus ventured forth upon the asphalt, and finding a foothold of sorts, began to advance slowly across the road. He paused every few inches to reassure himself that all was well. The warmth of the sun was pleasant, and he took his time to savor the gentle heat of the asphalt. As he moved forward across the yellow mark at the crown of the road, his body was stretched out almost straight with only small undulations to move himself forward.

Since he, like all his fellows, had no sense of hearing, he was totally unaware of the enemy hurtling toward him at more than a hundred feet a second until suddenly his startled eyes caught a glimpse of a blurred mass almost upon him. In a single movement of incredible speed, the straight body whipped into a coil, the head raised and drawn back, ready for instant striking.

The action saved him as the wheels pounded over the asphalt exactly where his head had been. So great was the speed of the cycle that when Crotalus struck out, the enemy was already past him.

Galvanized by the realization of his complete vulnerability in this alien space away from his usual cover, Crotalus began to crawl frantically toward the distant rocks and bushes that lay beyond the road. He was unaware that the enemy had cut his engine, braked to a stop, and was even now turning around in the road beyond.

At the edge of the road, Crotalus paused before crawling down into the ditch. As he did, he saw the enemy slowly rolling toward him. He redoubled his efforts and plunged down into the bottom of the ditch, then started up the other side to reach the cover beyond. The loose soil was his undoing. It prevented any rapid progress; he climbed three inches and slid back two. He reached the top and started across the short stretch of clear ground to the shelter of the brush beyond, but he was too late. The enemy had dismounted and was upon him.

Crotalus had no choice but to turn and face his pursuer. He coiled his long body tightly, his flat, triangular head drawn back to strike. His tail buzzed sharply and intensely like dry seeds shaken rapidly in a paper bag.

The enemy stayed out of reach but tormented Crotalus by tossing small stones at him. Crotalus held his ground until the enemy turned away to find larger stones. At this, Crotalus began to move rapidly toward the brush with fear urging his nerves and muscles into all the speed he could muster. He was into the brush and headed for the shelter of a space beneath a large stone under a sagebrush. He never made it.

The enemy tossed a large stone which smashed down beside him. He coiled again to face this renewed threat. A second stone landed squarely upon him so that the nether half of his body was pinned immobile to the ground. Crotalus instinctively struck at the rock, at the air, at the rock again. Terror so seized him that he was able to thrash about and dislodge the stone enough to pull his body loose. When he summoned his strength to move away, he discovered that the stone had broken his back so that only part of him had locomotion; the rest dragged behind, a useless appendage—a brake that prevented more than a suggestion of forward movement.

The enemy came close again, but Crotalus found himself too stricken to coil. As he feebly struck out at the feet of the towering, black shape above him, a stone fell upon him and smashed his head so that he knew terror and fear no more.

The enemy placed a heavy boot upon the mangled head and, with a deft stroke of a sharp blade he carried, removed the ten rattles from the tail and tossed them to his mate—crowded close to watch the trophy-taking. Then the enemy hung the still-twitching body upon a branch of sagebrush. As the engine roared into life again, the enemy looked once more with a sort of atavistic satisfaction at the lifeless shape hanging on the sagebrush and then accelerated down the road toward Wildrose in a rising crescendo of sound.

As quiet returned, the ebbing sun lit the gently swaying body in a warm light. The beautiful turquoise patch at the throat was brilliant, except where streaks of blood from the ruined head had stained it.

In the distance, the burros that had watched the drama in placid wonder went back to feeding on the dry browse; the black-throated sparrows once more hopped from bush to bush in search of twigs and scraps. The rough-legged hawk high in the sky above circled once more and then disappeared over the high ridges to the east.

*Buds of the prickly pear open in springtime to flower
behind a protective barrier of fierce spines.*

OVERLEAF: *Beyond the washes where creosote bush and jumping cholla send down roots
in search of water, harsh volcanic ridges rise bare against the sky.*

49

As winter rains fall, the saguaro grow fat with moisture;
when days grow warmer with the coming of summer,
creamy blossoms burst forth on every limb.

Ripe fruit grows thick and colorful among the sharp gray spines that give the grizzled senita its common name, "old man cactus." Sometimes the pleated green arms of the senita (left) show patches of red and white, a living mosaic in the desert.

In the early light of morning, black-throated sparrows perch on the clumps of cholla to send their song upon the day.

Desert lizards show a marked family resemblance to the giant dinosaurs that once lived here;
they are voracious predators, alert for any insect that dares approach too close.

Mound cactus takes a tenacious hold upon the rock of desert hills, its blossoms
a beacon for every wandering bee or humming bird that passes by.

Barrel cactus grows on rocky slopes
where moisture lies hidden beneath
the surface; its spines form
a cross-hatched maze to fend off
browsers and protect its stem
from the fierce sun.

Showy blooms of the staghorn cholla distract the unwary
from the cruel barbs that hide beneath.

The beavertail cactus draws on water stored
in its fat, green stems to send forth a crown
of pink flowers in the desert's early heat,
whereas the desert lily (right) must rely
on the moisture in its bulb to sustain
its lovely flower through a short life.

Sheltered by the same shell his ancestors wore
eons ago, the desert tortoise makes his unhurried
rounds in search of succulent leaves.

Prince's plume grows tall and thick
in the dry washes of the Mojave,
far below the moisture reserves
of the Sierra Nevada's snowy crest.

Desert primroses and great clumps of yellow desert senna
find a lean but uncrowded living in the dunes;
here, too, is the ubiquitous astragalus, its pods betraying
its membership in the pea family.

*In spring the yucca sends up tall stalks of creamy blossoms,
yellow-splashed blackbirds make their nests in salt cedar
thickets along the Colorado, and the palo verde wraps itself
in a cloud of yellow flowers, here almost hiding a saguaro
that for more than a century has lived in the old tree's shelter.*

In southern Sonora, where the
central Mexican thorn forest meets
the cactus desert of the north,
butterflies rest like yellow leaves
upon the twigs, and locusts
masquerade as bright seedpods
tucked among the leafy branches.

Among the rewards for those willing
to explore the hot Sonoran countryside
at close range are tiny fishhook cactus that
grow only an inch or two above the ground
and little pods that hang on dried vines
like gay Japanese lanterns.

Little grows on the salt-laden playas of the northern Mojave, but on the slopes above, wild descendants of burros abandoned by miners a century ago find browse in natural pastures.

OVERLEAF: *Far to the south, down the long peninsula of Baja California, one still finds the familiar silhouette of yucca, bending before the winds that blow in unbroken from the wide Pacific.*

71

LIGHTLY UPON THE LAND

Man has been in these deserts almost since the time when, millennia ago, the first Asiatics crossed from Siberia into Alaska and began long migrations south to land's end at Tierra del Fuego. Why some of them chose to settle here no one knows, though when the first men arrived, these lands were far less arid that now. Later arrivals probably fled aggressive neighbors who drove them from more favored lands north and east. There is persuasive evidence that others migrated north from civilizations more advanced in Mesoamerica.

For whatever reason, they came here early and hunted the game that abounded; the record of their occupancy is as ancient as any in the New World. In one cave deep within the Papago homeland is litter left behind by ancient hunters some eleven thousand years ago. On bare mesas near Blythe are huge figures laid out in stone upon the ground, as meticulously ordered as any white horse that the ancients carved into the chalk cliffs of Wiltshire in England. At Naco, along the Arizona-Sonora border, scholars have uncovered the skeleton of a mammoth with the spear points that brought him down, evidence of the antiquity of those hunters.

Throughout the desert one can find petroglyphs, cryptic inscriptions that could have some hidden tribal or religious meaning or could be nothing more than Stone Age graffiti. In caves, on mounds of rock, on sheltered cliff faces, they stand in mute ranks, an undeciphered language.

Whatever edifices were built have, for the most part, vanished under the onslaught of wind and water. Only the superstructure of the most recent, Casa Grande, exists in any appreciable measure of its original state. All the rest are mounds in the desert, rich in arrowheads and shattered pottery and vague legends.

Those ancients of the desert who lived in the saguaro lands of southern Arizona are called Hohokam by their descendants, who still live in the same valleys and hills. The more romantic among the whites have translated the name as "those who have vanished"; the more literal is "that which has been used up"—probably more apt, given the extremities of climate in which they found themselves.

They built elaborate towns with many structures—some for living, others for ritual. They built marvelously engineered canals to bring water upon their lands from the Gila and Salt and

Santa Cruz, a system almost as advanced in concept as any that followed centuries later; they cultivated several species of corn, a plant developed by the civilizations of the distant Mexican altiplano. And sunken ball courts point to a connection with civilizations a thousand miles away in central Mexico.

These early men probably came north from what is now southern Sinaloa and Nayarit, bearing an advanced culture with them. (All evidence points to the fact that both Aztec and Hohokam came from common stock.)

Artifacts they left behind in the ruins of their ancient cities leave no doubt as to their artistry. They were expert basket makers and potters. They were the first of mankind to learn the etching process; they used weak acid from cactus juice to etch designs in shells from the far ocean five hundred years before Renaissance man in Italy stumbled upon the method.

They were one of several high cultures in the New World, cultures made possible by the discovery of agriculture with its fixed locations—Peru, Guatemala, and Yucatan; the plateau of Mexico; and the valleys of the Ohio, where the Hopewellian culture thrived. In the American Southwest there were the Anasazi in Mesa Verde, Canyon de Chelly, and a hundred other cliff side communities; the Mogollon along the rimrock country in Arizona and New Mexico; the Hohokam in the arid lands to the south.

All their towns were abandoned about the same time early in the fifteenth century. The reason, no one knows for certain. Dendrochronologists counting growth rings of ancient trees point to signs of a major drought of long duration a century earlier throughout the Southwest. There are other theories. No matter—the towns were abandoned, and the people dispersed.

By the time European men appeared, descendants of the Hohokam were living in several tribes scattered about the desert. All but two quickly disappeared under the impact of the advancing alien culture. One surviving tribe of the Hohokam, living in harsh mountains just north of the present international border, called themselves *tohono au'autam*, the Desert People. Other Indians called them *pavi coatam*, the Bean Eaters. Imprecise and careless Spanish ears perverted this into Papago, a name they bear to this day. Their cousins along the Gila and the Salt suffered a similar treatment. Their name for themselves was *akimel au'autam*, the River People. Some Spaniards coming among them for the first time asked what the tribe was called; some tribesman, misunderstanding, answered with a word having a negative meaning. To this day, the tribe to outsiders bears the name the Spanish gave them in error—*pima*, a negative reply to a misunderstood question.

The Pima were advanced agriculturists. They cultivated lands along the Gila and Salt; to bring water to distant fields, they constructed marvelously engineered canals of great length and capacity, canals of proper gradient to conduct water across miles of desert. Their farms prospered so that when white Americans first passed this way a century ago on their way to the Pacific, the Pima fields were the granaries that replenished their stores and made the passage possible.

On the whole they were a peaceful people—but like most Indians, warfare with neighboring tribes was a natural custom. Their eastern neighbors, the Apache, were more warlike than most; indeed, they enjoyed it. They made it a workable way of life, stealing food from the Pima and Papago and frequently seizing their women. When the Spanish first invested the valley of the Rio Grande east of the Apache strongholds in the sixteenth century, they brought soldiers to beat back these marauders.

In this effort they were moderately successful, but they also brought an unexpected asset to the Apache—horses. Afoot, the Apache was fearsome enough; mounted upon a horse, he was almost invincible. The desert tribes were hard put to fend him off.

When Padre Kino first came to the desert with his company a century later, he was met by Pima and Papago making signs that Kino thought to be an invitation to preach and baptize. The chances are equally as good that these Indians had heard about the priests along the Rio Grande who had Spanish soldiers to fight the Apache and welcomed Kino and his military supporters not as evangelists but as bulwarks against their enemy.

Most of this warfare against the Apache was retaliatory—the Pima preferred not to start wars. Yet the bounty of their fields made them an inviting target for Yavapai from the hills to the north as well as Apache from their eastern borders. When they did fight, the Pima fought well. They were as cruel in war as any other Indians. They scalped the fallen, taking no male prisoners, and often sold captured women and children into slavery in Mexico.

Their greatest battle grew out of a case of hospitality and friendship to another tribe. A band of Maricopa, a Yuman tribe living near the confluence of the Colorado and the Gila, grew tired of fighting and losing battles with their aggressive cousins nearby. They moved off upriver and eventually came to Pima lands. There they sought shelter and were given land to call their own just west of the Pima settlements. They remained to cultivate the earth, gather seeds from the desert plants, and hunt the rabbits that were a major part of their diet.

All was peaceful until the year 1858 when a large Yuman war party came up the river seeking the defecting Maricopa. They found them, fell upon their outlying settlements, and devastated them. The surviving Maricopa drew together for defense and sent messengers to the Pima requesting help.

The Pima responded—war parties came from Sacaton and Blackwater and Bapchule, from Casa Blanca and all the other Pima towns. They assembled on the Maricopa lands and fell upon the Yuma with great ferocity. When the war cries died away, and the dust had settled, only one Yuma brave remained alive, feigning death to escape detection. After night fell he rose and limped his way westward for many days until he came to where the people of his tribe were camped beside the Colorado. He told them the news of the battle. The women wailed for their dead; the old men fell silent. The Yuma never marauded again. The Pima never fought another battle, nor was there any need. The Yavapai were impressed by such prowess in battle, and the Apache were too busy hiding from the United States cavalry.

After the Apache were suppressed, Cochise dead, and Geronimo carted off to end his days behind bars at Fort Sill in Oklahoma Territory, the Pima lived out their lives peaceably beside the free-flowing Salt and Gila. They tilled their farms and fished the waters of the rivers. When white men came to live, they made them welcome. These latecomers settled upstream, broke the land, and loosed their cattle to forage among scant desert grasses. They took a leaf from the Indians' book and began to irrigate their lands. Some of these canals even today are those the Hohokam built a thousand or more years ago. But where the Pima had merely used temporary diversion dams to turn aside the rivers into the desert, the white men built permanent dams to impound the water. The Salt and Gila no longer flowed free; the Indians found them bone dry when they reached Pima lands.

Through the years the Pima got the short end of the stick. In wet years, they got what water the white farmers didn't need; in dry years they got none at all. Farming became more difficult; life became precarious. Many Indians left their ancestral lands to live in poverty in the white men's towns; those left on the land farmed as best they could or existed on handouts from the government.

Times are a little better now. There is always water for the Pima farms—not enough but sufficient that there is seldom hunger. Pima men still leave their lands to work in the white men's fields near Coolidge and Chandler and Phoenix. And little by little, younger men forget the old ways. Only very old wise men know the dim legends and the ancient ways. Only a few can still read the calendar stick to recall past glories of the tribe.

Yet the influence of days that are gone still casts a spell. On a rough road that runs beyond Bapchule, there is a natural amphitheater formed by a depression between two low, cactus-covered hills. No one goes here en route to somewhere else. The occasional Indian comes to pay his respects to the spirit that lives here.

In the center of the amphitheater is a mound that marks the grave of an old wise man. No one knows how long ago he died or who he was. Around his grave are low stone walls, three in number, with a gap at each of the cardinal points of the compass—gates to allow his spirit to pass freely. Atop his grave is a granite boulder, brought here from some distant rocky slope by men who had no idea of the wheel.

In a hollowed-out place atop the boulder are small offerings of value—a coin, an old brass key, an ancient arrowhead, the casing of a rifle bullet. Young men come here to ask advice in matters of the heart, and old men to seek solace from a revered elder gone on.

In time such holy places may disappear completely. The calendar stick will pass when there are no gnarled fingers to rub its carved length and recall events recounted there; the ancient legends will die out with no one to remember them. That time may be almost upon the tribe. To the young men, the culture of the internal combustion engine seems more important.

Those cousins of the Pima, Papago who live in waterless mountains to the south, have had a more precarious existence. They have no rivers in their lands, save where a small band lives within sight of Tucson along the channel of the Santa Cruz. The main body of the tribe lives along the Arizona-Sonora border in a large reservation; only the Navajo in the canyon country have more land. Unlike many other tribes who were removed from their homelands and herded into lands not wanted by expanding white civilization, the lands of Papago and Pima are their ancestral lands. Their forefathers, the Hohokam, left villages all over the present-day reservations.

These tribesmen in an older time were completely at the mercy of capricious rains that fell sporadically upon their lands. They lived permanently in the mountains where there were small springs and seeps that never dried up completely. When summer rains fell, they made their way down to bajadas where cloudbursts had left a legacy of moist earth and had filled to overflowing the *charcos,* small depressions where water collected after the rains—drinking water for the tribe. They planted their corn and beans and melons on these damp bajadas and tended them until they ripened. When the crops were harvested and the charcos turned to dust, they withdrew to the little waters in the hills.

Because there were years when the rains came

not at all or brought so little moisture that crops on the bajadas died before they ripened, the Papago were wise in ways of living upon the land. They knew the value of every plant that prospered in the desert. They cut the heart from the agave and roasted it; they gathered seed from mesquite and ironwood; they collected fruit from cholla and saguaro and from it made jellies, preserves, and wine for the sacred summer ceremonies of the tribe. To this day the Papago journey to the saguaro camps in the hills to gather the ripe, red fruit—a high occasion of the tribal year. And since the month they gather the fruit is near the end of the annual dry season when food grew scarce, they called it the Saguaro Harvest Moon; it marked the beginning of the new year.

They sent their strongest and swiftest men on a two-hundred mile run to the shores at the head of the distant gulf to gather salt for the tribe—or so the story goes. In truth, the trek was made to entice the storm clouds that live on the gulf in summer to follow them back to bring rain upon Papago lands. They succeeded often enough for men to have lived in these baked hills for thousands of years—tribute to the persuasiveness of those sent to summon the rain god who lived in the clouds.

They had one tremendous thing working in their favor—their ancestral lands were so uninviting that white men never entertained ideas of usurping them. So, except for some scattered mining that petered out for the most part, the Papago were able to live undisturbed save for an occasional Apache foray. There were no battles over river water; the tribe had none to begin with. Probably this lack of serious contention throughout the years is the reason the Papago feels much less animosity toward white men than do more distant and militant tribes like Sioux and Navajo and Cheyenne.

They have their ancient shrines, too, as do their Pima kin. In a wash near Santa Rosa is a hidden cairn—a pile of flat, gray rocks some two feet high. Instead of stone walls surrounding the rocks, there is a tall fence of spiny ocotillo branches, a fence with traditional openings to east and south, west and north. Frequently, at some time of renewal, the old stakes are removed and new ones put in their place. The old ones are stacked atop the branches of other years in two long piles five or more feet high on each side of the stone markers.

Legend has it that at one time a drought of great duration came upon the land, and the well that was here in the wash grew dry; no amount of deepening would bring forth water. Sages of the tribe were consulted; these men read the signs and interpreted the circumstances as manifestations of the displeasure of the rain god. They picked out two young children and threw them into the deep pit to mollify the deity. There is no record of whether rains came or not. There are certain of the Papago who still hear, when conditions are sympathetic, the cries of the two children coming from beneath the sands.

To me there seems to be a corollary between Papago hurling these victims into the dry well and ancient Maya selecting a virgin to be thrown into the cenote in Chichén Itzá in distant Yucatan. In either case, the purpose was identical—to propitiate the rain god upon whom both cultures were so dependent.

No one knows how far back into the past this happened, but the knowledge is certain that it happened a long, long time ago. The bottoms of the piles of ocotillo staves beside the stones have long since returned to dust—and decay is slow in these lands.

The lands of the Papago are those where the Jesuit evangelist Eusebio Kino established the northernmost of a string of missions, stretching from present-day Magdalena and Caborca north almost to Tucson where stands lovely San Xavier del Bac, the White Dove of the Desert. Most of these Indians are Catholic, a legacy of those early religious workers almost three centuries ago. The missions in the north were abandoned when the Jesuit fathers withdrew on orders of the monarch in Madrid. For a time Franciscans took their places, but when Mexico threw off the heavy hand of Spain, the missions were secularized and the Franciscans left, too. The Papago, cut adrift from the hierarchy by the fluctuations of politics, kept the faltering flame of their religion burning, celebrating the sacraments as best they could remember how during a century of neglect.

When missionaries returned again in the early days of this century under the banner of the Franciscans, they found small edifices surmounted by rude crosses in each village. Pagan rites were mixed with half-remembered Christian ceremonies—the Sonora Catholic Church. To this day they still exist, outside the Roman discipline but tolerated by the brown-robed fathers. They use ikons of a sort instead of statues; on the walls of these tiny chapels are religious photographs and clippings from newspapers and magazines. There are plastic flowers from Japan upon the altar, a particular weakness among the Papago. Candles cast a faint glow, and there is sometimes the smell of strange incense.

In the established churches and missions, the Papago claim a proprietary interest. These are churches belonging to the Indians; the white priests are merely transitory servants of God tarrying for a time. The padre at one of the missions much frequented by tourists told of the time when the Papago sexton informed him that men of the parish were coming for a ceremony of purification of their church and that it might be best to absent himself for a time—a suggestion that barely veiled the implied imperative. Being wise in the ways of the Papago, he found duties to take him to a neighboring parish. But an underling, a young priest, hid himself within the confessional to see what would happen.

He saw the Indian men enter the church carrying stiff brooms made of tule rushes; the handles were hollow canes long enough to reach the ceiling. While an incantation was offered by a medicine man of the tribe, the brooms were raised aloft to briskly sweep all the corners and crannies of the sanctuary. Attached to the bottom of each hollow cane was a tin can. As evil spirits were dislodged, they fell down through the hollow broom handles into the tin cans below. When the ceremony was completed, the Indians took away the evil spirits captive in the cans to some distant place and buried them, covered over with spiny cholla joints and heavy stones to bar their escape—as efficacious a way as any to purify the premises. The young priest came forth from his hiding place a wiser man than when he entered.

They are a friendly people who enjoy life in spite of the rigors of their surroundings. They visit back and forth a great deal, a habit that goes back beyond antiquity. They are a stocky, heavyset people with a tendency toward obesity, a tendency augmented by the tribe's embracing Mexican tortillas and frijoles as a staple of their diet and white men's introduction of the can opener. They move slowly; this, combined with their bulk, has sometimes led white men to accuse them of being lazy. This view says more about the white men's obtuseness than about the Papago's character. For laziness was a trait these desert dwellers could not afford. Merely wresting a livelihood from the hills and valleys of their homeland was hard and constant work—harder than most latecomers from more easy lands could imagine. The Papago moves slowly because he is decorous and dignified and because there is no reason to hurry. Indeed, when a Papago urges his horse into a gallop his brothers consider him drunk, unless he is chasing a calf or a steer. There would be no other reason.

He lives now in permanent villages upon the floor of the desert far from the seeps and springs in the hills. He lives where he does because the government drilled wells in the desert and pumped water for the villages. Except for a few old men, no longer does he plant his beans and corn and squash upon the bajadas following the summer rains; no longer does he make the long trek to the gulf for salt. He buys his beans and corn and iodized salt from the trading post at inflated prices.

Some of them raise cattle for the general market. Most of them work as field hands on white men's farms beyond the reservation or in the copper mines at Ajo or for the Bureau of Indian Affairs. Some are on permanent relief. Most of them have forgotten the old ways—the gathering of seeds, the snaring of wild game. Only the saguaro harvest remains as a food-gathering activity of the tribe. They no longer make pottery—they use plastic pans and buckets from the trading post. Probably the only skill being passed on from generation to generation is the art of making fine Papago baskets—not for any need of them but rather because white men will pay well for them. Women who make baskets and cattlemen are probably the only free enterprisers of the tribe.

The Papago is almost completely dependent on white men's technology—for water, for power, for transportation and communication, for jobs. Should these be cut off, he would be hard put to fend for himself until he could re-learn lost skills.

Most of the water on Papago lands is pumped water—fossil water that collected there thousands of years ago when this was a gentler place of lakes and flowing streams. It is finite, not replaced by summer rains percolating into the earth. Should the Papago pump it out of the ground as fast as his white neighbors are doing, he will pump himself back into his father's condition—waterless, except for what seeps from the hills or falls briefly from storm clouds in summer.

A scholar who knows more about these desert tribes than they themselves know has said that they were able to exist within the desiccated boundaries of their homeland for two millennia or more because they rested "lightly upon the land."

And there's the tragedy of it—they abandon old ways that sustained them for a thousand years to emulate a culture that never rested lightly upon any land. When the white man exhausts the stores of waters within these deserts, once again he will move on to other lands leaving ruin behind him. And the Papago and his cousins will be left within a sterile land, lacking native skills to sustain themselves.

Below the border near the coast in mid-desert lives a tribe that neither the Spaniards nor the Mexicans ever really vanquished. The fierce Yaqui, who lived along the river that bore their name, were more than a match for the colonizers. So warlike and formidable were they that advancing waves of Spaniards and Mexicans parted and passed around them. All attempts to subjugate them were met with fierce resistance. In the eighteenth century, warfare between the government and the tribe grew to such proportions that every able-bodied Yaqui took to the hills north of their lands and bloodied the troops sent against them. For years they stood off the enemy, but superior opposing numbers and armaments and eventual starvation did them in, and they were overcome.

Thousands of the survivors, whole families and entire villages, were shipped off in chains to Oaxaca and Puebla, to the henequen fields of Yucatan, to work in permanent exile.

The remnants of the tribe were herded back onto lands along the Yaqui River. As time went on, others coveted their rich lands; they lost more and more. Sporadic fighting went on, but the Yaqui never gave in. They kept their tribe pure. (Some of them fled persecution by crossing the border; there are today pure Yaqui communities in Phoenix and Tucson and Eloy, and other small enclaves as far away as California.) Along the river, they fought back stubbornly against all attempts to absorb them, resorting to force of arms when they had to, until 1928 when a truce was struck that still prevails. Even so, the government takes no chances; a battalion of troops is garrisoned in their midst to insure tranquillity.

Today, twenty-five thousand or more strong, they live along the north bank of the Río Yaquí. All about them are bountiful fields that the factory farmers of Mexico have made as prosperous as the Imperial and San Joaquin valleys of California. They resist all efforts to modernize their own agriculture; they plant their fields as they have done for a thousand years—to fill their needs and no more.

The only exception is the cultivation of wheat, planted in the fall when fields would ordinarily lie fallow and harvested in late spring just before planting time for all other crops. They sell this small yield of wheat for cash, as it does not form part of their diet. This small profit is all the cash that many of them ever possess.

They no longer grow cotton, although the first Spaniards found them growing enough for their own needs. Now it is left for the Mexican farmers who grow large acreages as a sole cash crop. Yaqui do not look upon such monoculture as being what a man should do. His independence, his self-sufficiency would be compromised by such farming. He would have to buy his food—a thing not to be done.

So he plants his fields, hoping for water in his dry irrigation ditches or carrying water to his fields from hand-dug wells, and harvests whatever survives drought, insects, marauding cows, and burros. The cactus-thorn forest that surrounds him provides a supplement to the yield from his fields. He knows every edible plant that grows in the desert.

The pressure grows each year upon the Yaqui to adapt the ways of the rest of Mexico but they will not. They stand defiant—and only they and the small tribe of Seri along the northern shores of the Sea of Cortez have stood against the waves of conquest. All the others have been absorbed in the tide of Hispano-Mexican dominance. On a trip last year through northern Sonora in what was Indian country at the time of the Spaniard's coming, questions concerning the whereabouts of the aboriginal population brought the same answer everywhere: *"No hay indios aquí."*

So only these two desert tribes of the south retain their identity; along with the tribes living north of the border, only these remain of the people who rested lightly upon the land. Perhaps even the remaining few have an uncertain future; pressures upon them and upon the land they hold may become too much. If it should happen and they too should disappear, something irreplaceable would be gone, and we would all be diminished by the loss.

indian peoples

Weathered signs point the way to Papago villages (overleaf); along the roads are shrines to honor the Virgin and crosses to mark where Indians have died in the wreckage of automobiles.

Scattered through Papago lands are well-kept ceremonial houses of traditional Indian architecture, for use when saguaro fruit is made into wine for religious rites.

In outlying Papago settlements are structures built as their ancestors,
the Hohokam, built them a thousand years ago . . .

. . . of clay and straw and ocotillo staves; only plastic flowers
and store-bought clothes are a concession to modern times.

Angelic dark-eyed children
and dogs of scrambled ancestry
play in every Indian village, . . .

. . . and old men wise in
the knowledge of many years
take their ease in the warm
winter sunshine.

Among these desert tribes
there are still old medicine men
whose ancient eyes have seen
things that most have not.

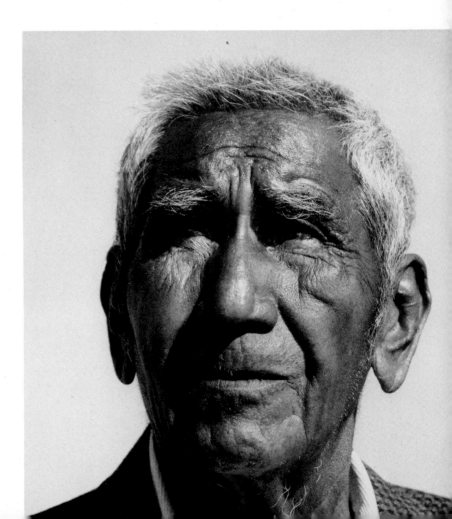

*Today some Papago occupy concrete-block houses erected
by the government; others still live in traditional shelters.*

Trees planted by Father Kino and the missionaries who followed have, in three centuries, grown as worn and weathered as the adobe buildings they shade.

Some of the early mission churches have the look of Europe, with ornate stonework, huge bell towers, and wide plazas drowsing in the sun. . . .

. . . But the churches of the Papago are pure Indian, temples in which
the Great Spirit and the Catholic God may dwell as one.

The desert is not kind to those of man's monuments that go long untended;
wind-blown sand gnaws at them incessantly and wears them away.

Sun, wind, and an occasional
cloudburst weather the old
frame buildings mercilessly until
they are at best only reflections
of better days that are not
likely to come again.

OVERLEAF: *High up in the dry
ranges of the northern Mojave
lie the remains of mines
that once brought fortune-seekers
by the thousands, yielded riches
by the millions, then subsided
into lonely ruins.*

BRIEF ENTRADA

The reason that Pima and Papago, Maricopa and Mojave, Cocopah and Cahuila, Yuma and Yavapai were able to exist as tribal entities instead of disappearing under the onslaught of Hispanic conquest was that they lived on the northern borders of a fierce desert—a natural barrier between them and the Spanish provincial capital at Culiacán below the Río Sinaloa.

In 1529, less than ten years after Cortez conquered Tenochtitlán and made it his capital, Nuño de Guzmán, as cruel and ruthless a man as Spain ever numbered among its conquistadores, crossed over the Sierra de Tepic and made his way northward up the coastal plain, setting torch and sword to every Indian village he found. By 1531, he had reached the site of what is now the Sinaloan capital, Culiacán.

During his campaign, he seized thousands of Indians and sent them south into slavery in Jalisco, Michoacán, and the lands surrounding Mexico City, while Aztecs and Tarascans of those lands were brought north and forced into servitude in Sinaloa. These various tribal Indians interbred with each other, with the whites, and to a lesser degree with black slaves brought by the Spaniards. Immediately, ancient cultures began to disappear, and a mestizo race emerged. Such was the Spanish policy of subjugation, and it was eminently successful.

The harsh and perilous desert was encountered a little to the north of Culiacán. Here Guzmán halted, convinced that the land which lay beyond had little to enrich the Spanish crown or the fortunes of the conquistadores. For many years, only expeditions crossed the desert into lands of the north. When Cabeza de Vaca stumbled into Culiacán in 1536 after making his way for eight long years from the Gulf of Mexico through the desert to this Spanish outpost, he brought startling tales of the riches of Cíbola that triggered a series of expeditions. Fray Marcos de Niza, Francisco de Ulloa, Francisco Vásquez de Coronado, and Melchior Díaz went north seeking treasure. When they returned with accounts of great, empty wastelands and poor Indian hovels, the Spaniards turned their backs upon the Sonoran desert north of the Río Sinaloa and for the most part abandoned any attempt to colonize or exploit it.

Almost at the same time, an attempt was being made to explore and colonize Baja California so that a port of call could be secured there for treasure galleons en route from Manila to Acapulco. One attempt after another ended in failure; the only immediate result was that, probably as a result of the introduction of the white man's diseases, most of the Indians of the peninsula simply disappeared, vanished as if they had never existed.

The Spaniards fared not much better and after a century and a half abandoned further attempts at settlement and left it in the hands of a few dedicated Jesuits. Over three centuries, a few settlements grew up around the missions in oases in the desert but not until the last decade of modern times has there been a new impetus toward colonization to make room for the crowded Mexicans of the mainland.

But early in this commerce between the mainland and the peninsula, the Spaniards established small ports where major rivers entered the gulf or where natural harbors existed—on the Río Fuerte, the Río Yaquí, and at the great bay where Guaymas Indians lived.

When Coronado made his expedition northward in 1540, he took large herds of cattle with him as a food supply for the journey. As his column went up through the valleys of the Sierra Madre, many animals escaped from the vaqueros and remained behind to roam these grasslands. Within a century, there were thousands of wild cattle in the hills and mountains bordering the desert; a cattle industry that persists to this day slowly developed there, established by Spaniards pushing northward, seeking silver and gold in these ranges.

The effect of Spanish settlement on the Indians of these hills was catastrophic. They were seized and pressed into slavery in the mines and on the encomiendas. Their treatment was miserable, and they died in droves because of starvation and abuse and disease. When the supply of hill Indians was depleted, soldiers went down into the plains and seized those living on the desert. The rapidity with which a tribe disappeared was in direct proportion to its docility. The most gentle vanished quickly, transported from their homes to labor under the whips of alien overseers. In most cases only the strong survived. Their women were seduced or raped or married by the Hispano-Mexicans. The rest of the Indians simply disappeared, replaced by mestizos, the new Mexicans. The tribes of the southern desert— Opata, Guasave, Suaqui, Sinaloa, Pima Bajo, Sisibotani, and a score more—exist only as forgotten names mentioned in the sparse histories of this place and those times.

By the end of the seventeenth century, the lands of the Sierra Madre and its foothills were thinly held and colonized by Spanish and Mexican ranchers and miners, almost to the point of where the international border lies today. Here they were stopped by an obstacle as effective as any the Spanish ever encountered in the New World—Apache who looked upon these lands as solely their own and who swore blood vengeance upon any interlopers.

The Spanish entrada had reached the high-water mark of its penetration into northwestern Mexico—the arid lands north and west of Culiacán saw no great numbers of them. Even the priests who pressed on confined their efforts to the more favored lands, establishing their missions most often in the foothills where the living was easier than in the desert; they followed the mines and ranches that were being established. In time there were thirty-five missions in Sinaloa and southern Sonora. And the process of Mexicanization of the tribes kept pace with them. Through interbreeding with whites and blacks or enslavement in the mines, most of the Indians vanished, and mestizos took their place.

It was left to a band of Jesuits—most of them bearing Italian, German, and Bohemian names—to carry the flag and the cross to the northern desert where no European had been seen since the first explorers had passed by a century and a half before. And even they kept to the edges of the desert, in valleys whose rivers rose in the mountains and ran down to disappear beneath the dry sands of the desert. These valleys were verdant enough, with trees and grassy meadows for shade and forage.

The captain of these Jesuits and their attendant soldiers and retainers was a native of Trent near the Austro-Italian border. His family name was Chino, but since this in Spanish implied that its owner was Chinese, the good padre changed its spelling and went down in history as Eusebio Francisco Kino of the Company of Jesus. No name in the history of the southwestern desert has greater luster.

He established his string of missions in what the government in Mexico City had long called Pimería Alta, the upper lands of the Pima. He brought seeds to the tribes for planting, he gave them horses and cattle, and he offered them salvation. Above all, he extended a mantle of protection over them against the rapacious Spaniards and Mexicans in the hill country to the east who would have driven them into the mines to be worked to death had not Kino stood in the way.

This hardy man was not only an evangelist— he was a distinguished mathematician and astronomer, an explorer, a cartographer. He thought nothing of riding a hundred miles in two days, preaching and baptizing, taking time to explore new paths and noting his discoveries in his journals, diaries, and on his maps. He was idolized by the tribes of southern Arizona; he was the only white man who could ride alone among them over a thousand miles of desert without fear.

In the course of his wide-ranging travels, he rediscovered something that the first Spanish explorers knew but that succeeding generations had forgotten—that California was not an island. His discovery made possible Juan Bautista de Anza's two overland expeditions from Sonora, which established Monterey as the capital of Alta California.

Kino died in 1711 at the age of sixty-nine. He fell ill while attending the dedication of a new chapel at the Magdalena church. He lay down upon the only bed he had ever known in the Pimería—two Indian blankets spread upon the ground with his saddle for a pillow. He never rose again. They buried him at Magdalena, and his bones lay forgotten for more than two centuries. Recently they were discovered and put on display for tourists in the plaza before the church. Kino deserved better than this.

He was no ordinary man and never content with things as they were. He was always attracted by what lay *mas allá*—a little beyond: the search for what lay *mas allá* drove him until the day he died. His successors on the other hand, were seldom driven by such urges. His brother Jesuits were apparently content to work in the vineyard he had planted, for history does not record any expansion of the mission territories after Kino was gone.

The Jesuits were hard-working and successful. Their mission ranches prospered. Yet all they earned was ploughed back into building and rebuilding the missions, feeding the hungry Indians, and financing expeditions against the marauding Apache. Still, because they were in a place where gold and silver abounded, the suspicion arose that the Jesuits were amassing and hiding treasure in their churches. So strong grew this rumor, aided primarily by those who dis-

After two centuries the walls of Cocóspora still stand as monuments to the grace with which the mission fathers built.

liked the aggressiveness of the Jesuits, that it reached the ear of the viceroy in Mexico City and eventually the court in Madrid. In time, the rumor prospered and became fact in the mind of the king. In 1767, the word came down in royal decree; the Jesuits in the Pimería and Baja California were recalled to Mexico City and then banished from the land. For two centuries the search has gone on for their buried treasure; but there was no treasure.

To fill the vacuum left by the Jesuits, Franciscans from Querétaro came north and took over the missions, but at best they were caretakers. They never approached the successes of the Jesuits. Indeed, revolts broke out, priests were murdered, ranches and mines destroyed. The Franciscan priest who came closest to emulating Kino, Father Francisco Tomás Garcés, was beaten to death by Yuma along the Colorado.

There was great loss of life in the Pimería as Papago and Pima joined forces against the Hispano-Mexican culture and effectively stopped its further advance.

Not long after Mexico proclaimed its independence and threw out its Spanish rulers, the missions were secularized, the priests expelled, the churches abandoned. While dissident generals disrupted the central government with a century of jockeying for power, Sonora, far to the north, was left to its own devices. A long succession of self-aggrandizing governors there cared little about the empty desert to the north. It remained empty until the Americans took the northern portion from Mexico as war booty and began to colonize it during the great westward expansion of the mid-nineteenth century.

So the names on the maps today are seldom Spanish—only the rivers and mountains that the first conquistadores had noted on their charts. The rest are Indian—*ari sonac* ("small spring") and *tchoohk sonac* ("black spring")—or American—Thermal, Wickenburg, Salome, Barstow, Palm Springs, Daggett, and Quartzsite.

But after many decades the northern surge revived; thousands of Mexicans, the vast majority with more Indian blood than Spanish, came north seeking work in the American fields and stayed to become Americans themselves. Throughout the Sonoran Desert in Arizona and California, wherever agriculture has taken hold, the soft sound of Spanish is as prevalent as English; in some towns it is the only language.

And in the statehouse in Phoenix where for sixty years names like Ashurst, Hayden, Goldwater, and Fannin indicated where the power lay, names of Spanish origin now have joined them. The entrada—after a century and a half—continues.

There are many tales—some true, some apocryphal— about men long gone who roamed the roadless wastes between the Panamints, Superstitions, Tehachapis, and the Sierra Madre Occidental of northern Mexico. One such tale, in this case mostly true, concerns one Philip Tedro, a Greek who came to the desert from half a world away, from ancient Smyrna in Turkey.

His particular odyssey had its genesis when Edward F. Beale, a former naval officer who had served under Commodore Stockton during the seizure and subsequent occupation of California by American military forces, was sent East with Kit Carson in 1847 to Washington to carry official dispatches to the War Department. During the long and tedious journey, Beale had thought long about the difficulties in providing sufficient water and forage for the horses as they made their way eastward through the arid, dusty basins lying

between the Sierra Nevada and the Rocky Mountains. He convinced himself that the beast of burden of the Old World, the camel, would be perfectly at home in the Great Basin desert and in the Mojave and Arizona deserts as well.

Upon his arrival in Washington, he set out to convince the powers there of the merits of his idea. His persuasion must have been most eloquent; Senator Jefferson Davis of Mississippi, a man of great stature in the halls of the Capitol, became an immediate proponent of the plan, throwing the weight of his prestige and influence into an attempt to persuade Congress to appropriate funds necessary for the procurement of a herd of camels from Africa and the Levant for military use in the American Southwest.

Congress did not part with a dollar as easily in those days as in more recent times. It was not until 1855, after Davis had become secretary of war, that the members of Congress were able to surmount their suspicions and prejudices against such a strange and unprecedented request. As a rider to the regular army appropriation bill, the sum of $30,000 was appropriated for the experiment. Immediately Secretary Davis set plans in motion to procure and transport camels to America.

So it was that the navy ship the U.S.S. Supply was modified into something resembling a floating stable and departed for the Mediterranean in search of camels and dromedaries. After touching at Tunis, Alexandria, and Constantinople, the Supply put in at the Turkish port of Smyrna and took on the last of a cargo of thirty-nine reluctant camels. It was here in Smyrna that Philip Tedro presented himself to the officer-in-charge as being Hadji Ali, a highly qualified Syrian camel driver, ready, willing, and able to accompany the animals to their final destination in the Mojave. Syrian he was not, highly qualified camel driver he may not have been either, but so desperate was Tedro to reach the California goldfields that he would have represented himself as Allah descended to earth if it would have helped his cause with the Americans.

He had no luck—the roster of camel drivers was already full. He must have made an impression, however; he was immediately signed on when the same ship and crew returned in 1856 to pick up a second contingent of camels. Along with seven other Greeks, Turks, and Levantines, Hadji Ali was signed on as a camel driver and went aboard when the camels were loaded for the long voyage back to Indianola on the Texas Gulf Coast.

In due time, the camel caravan shuffled out of Indianola on the way to Fort Defiance, Arizona, starting point for the trek across the deserts to Fort Tejon in the Tehachapis of southern California. As the animals began to raise the Texas dust by their slow, measured plodding, they were sped onward by urgings in a half-dozen tongues of the eastern Mediterranean.

They made their way across the endless miles of Texas and New Mexico. The days passed almost without incident, except when the column met with conventional wagon trains. When horses approached the long line of humpbacked monstrosities, some with strangely bedecked humans aboard and camel bells tinkling softly, they fled, with wide eyes and flaring nostrils, overturning wagons and breaking harness as they went. After the placid camels had gone on, cursing teamsters and muleskinners would round up their frightened animals and beat them back into line. Small wonder that these men hated the camels and vowed to shoot them on sight, should opportunity present itself—an attitude that persisted as long as there were camels in the desert.

At some point along the trail before the desert proper was reached, some difference of opinion arose between the Americans and the cameleers. One report has it that back wages was the issue, another that they feared the rigors of the journey ahead. Probably more to the point was the account that circulated to the effect that these devout, abstaining sons of Muhammad had drunk too deeply of the vine and were somewhere in the brush sleeping off the effects when it came time for the column to break camp and move on. Whether wages, fear, or drunkenness was the issue, the Americans, with a "damn your eyes" attitude consigned the drivers to perdition and went on without them. Only Hadji Ali made the crossing with the camels. By this time the Americans, ever ready to change the unusual into the familiar, had come to call him Hi Jolly, and so he remained until his dying day and forever after.

At length the column came up out of the desert into the Tehachapi Range and arrived at Fort Tejon, its final destination. Hi Jolly, whose knowledge of American geography was less than rudimentary, was disheartened to learn that although he was indeed in California he was still several hundred long, weary miles from the Mother Lode. From teamsters and soldiers at Fort Tejon, he heard of gold strikes at Whiskey Flats, a rip-roaring, gunslinging, hell-for-leather settlement some fifty miles away. He was on the point of slipping away to make a dash for it when word came that Beale was going east across the desert. Perhaps after the fifteen-hundred-mile jaunt with his camels from Texas almost to the Pacific, Hi Jolly really had become an expert camel driver and felt a pride in his calling that overcame even the lure of gold. In any event, for whatever reasons he may have had, when the caravan departed, Hi Jolly went with it.

For the next three years Hi Jolly and his camels crisscrossed the desert, hauling supplies from one part to another. Once the camels went all the way to Fort Defiance in Navajo country and back to supply a survey party mapping a railroad route from Chicago to Los Angeles. Another frequent port of call was Fort Yuma in the sand dunes near the head of the Sea of Cortez.

During all these journeys through lands as hot as any on earth, Beale's belief in the adaptability of the camels was completely justified. Where horses faltered and fell, the camels plodded on, browsing as they went on the leaves of the creosote bush and bur sage, drawing on reserves of water stored in the fat-filled humps on their backs. Beale's reports on the success of the experiment were such that the secretary of war in 1859 requested funds for a thousand more camels. Threats of secession preoccupied Congress, and the request fell on deaf ears. In 1861, the camels were transferred to Los Angeles when the Civil War began.

There they stayed for a while, stabled in the yard of the quartermaster's office. Children in the neighborhood came often to visit. Hi Jolly and his friend Greek George, another camel driver, hung chains of silver bells on the animals, and the children rode about the streets of the pueblo to soft, tinkling sounds.

A tale is told of the time Hi Jolly wanted to attend a picnic that the German people of Los Angeles were holding in a shady grove in an arroyo beyond the town. The Germans had arrived on foot, in wagons, in buggies, on horseback.

As was the custom in those times, the feature of any such celebration was a speech, high-flown, patriotic, and exceedingly lengthy. As the speaker of the day neared the climax of his peroration, Hi Jolly appeared upon the scene, riding in a yellow cart drawn by a pair of sedate camels, caparisoned with bright trimmings and adorned with the customary tinkling bells.

The tethered horses, frightened as usual by the appearance and scent and sound of the new arrivals, broke loose and bolted down the arroyo scattering picnic baskets for miles along the wash. The picnic speech ended abruptly with maledictions heaped upon Hi Jolly and his camels. The Germans walked home, hungry and angry; Hi Jolly turned his placid team around and drove back to the camel yard, the bells on the animals playing a sad dirge to match his mood.

By 1864, complaints from townsmen and ranchers, tired of having their horses and mules panic at the sight of camels, had risen to such a pitch that the government decided to dispose of them. Consequently they were driven overland to San Francisco and sold at auction. Some were sold to a moth-eaten traveling circus; others ended up hauling supplies to mines in the desert regions beyond the Sierra. Hi Jolly and Greek George found employment with these caravans plodding back and forth between the mining camps.

It was there on one of the lonely trails that Hi Jolly came as close as he ever came to making his fortune in gold. He met along the trail one day an affable Chinese gentleman desirous of buying salt, a commodity with which Hi Jolly's camels were laden at that time. A bargain was struck, large bags of salt exchanged for a small bag of gold dust. This bit of yellow dust became Hi Jolly's most treasured possession—that for which he had left his native Smyrna more than eight years before. He hefted it, examined it frequently, and took great pleasure in its possession.

One day when he was in a center of civilization, he decided to have his gold dust melted into a gold slug. He took it to a smelter where it was weighed, valued at $65, and a receipt given for it. On his next trip he went back to the smelter and was given a gold slug valued at $48. Enraged, he demanded the missing $17, a not inconsiderable sum in those days. Sadly he learned that he had been victimized. His smiling Chinese friend had filed a silver coin into dust, amalgamated it with the gold, and had passed a sack of dust that was three parts gold, one part silver.

As time went on, the packers and mule freighters objected so strenuously to the presence of the camels that their owner was forced to remove them from the mines. The entire herd, driven by Hi Jolly and Greek George, made the long overland march to Fort Yuma near the mouth of the Colorado where the owner hoped to sell them. When the caravan arrived at its destination, the owner promptly died, and the two camel drivers found themselves stranded with a number of hungry animals and no funds.

There was nothing for the two men to do except to turn the entire herd loose to forage in the desert to survive as best they could. Most of them lasted not long there. Muleteers and teamsters shot them on sight; Indians rounded up others and sold them to circuses and zoos. One camel, Topsy, lived to a ripe old age in the Griffith Park Zoo in Los Angeles and died there in 1934, seventy-eight years after making the first long trek from Texas to the desert.

The others vanished into the desert and became like

smoke and shadow. Reports persisted for years of an occasional humpbacked form drifting out of sight down some desert wash or disappearing into the heat waves of a desert mirage.

Hi Jolly fared not a great deal better. He made a spotty living on the fringes of the desert, either as a scout for an army tracking down the last recalcitrant Indians or as a packer moving supplies to some remote outpost. He took to wife in 1880 one Gertrude Serna, a lady who disappeared from recorded history as soon as the ceremony was entered in the marriage register of the Tucson church where the union was solemnized.

The rest of his life he spent in prospecting in the arid mountains that lie along the Colorado River in southwestern Arizona, searching for the gold that had led him to this desert years before. Probably he never saw more gold at one time than the little bagful the smiling Chinese had handed him on the trail years before.

There is a legend of his dying shortly after the turn of the century—as good a tale as any, and one which might even hold a grain of truth. A grizzled prospector rode into the town of Quartzsite in the Arizona desert and made his way into the only saloon in town. There he told a tale of having seen a big, red camel a few miles away in the desert. It could have been nothing else, he swore, but since these reports had been common currency in the desert for a quarter of a century he was neither believed nor disbelieved by those others leaning on the bar—save for one, an old and swarthy man who inquired as to where the prospector had seen the camel and upon being told, departed the premises.

A few days later they found the old man and the old, red camel both dead in the desert's bright winter sunlight, his arms wrapped around the camel's neck and his cheek peacefully resting against the still body—a tale in the finest tradition of the desert. Just because it didn't happen doesn't mean it isn't so.

So they brought him and laid him in a shallow, unmarked grave in the dusty cemetery at Quartzsite a few hundred feet away from where Interstate 10 nowadays climbs the long slope from the Colorado River, and the great trucks thunder by on their way to Phoenix. He lies there in the sparse shadow cast by a creosote bush. Years after he died, they raised a monument in the cemetery, a monument of stone from the hills he prospected. Inside the monument are the cremated remains of old Topsy, who outlived her master for thirty-one years, and sixty cents in coin, Hi Jolly's only wealth at the time of his death.

Atop the pyramidal monument is a replica of a standing camel. Below it is a tarnished brass plaque that simply says:

The Last Camp
of
HI JOLLY

Born somewhere in Syria
about 1828

DIED AT QUARTZSITE
December 16, 1903

Came to this country
February 10, 1856

CAMEL DRIVER, PACKER
SCOUT. OVER THIRTY
YEARS A FAITHFUL AID
TO THE U.S. GOVERNMENT

the dunes

*The undulating ridges
of sandy dunes repeat
endlessly patterns
of the desert mountains
from which they came.*

Desert winds shift dunes first this way,
then that, rippling them with tiny crests
like a restless moving sea.

In early sunlight shadows move across the dunes in great sweeping arcs, highlighting the ridges while the valleys still lie in darkness.

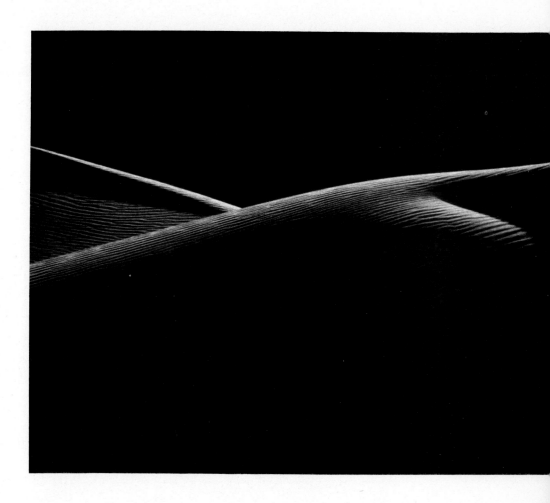

OVERLEAF: *After volcanic upheavals plants soon put down roots in the rich ash.*

PROSPECTORS AND OTHER HARDY SPECIES

Since European man first came upon the deserts of the American Southwest, the lure of hidden wealth has beckoned in a voice that has not yet been stilled. Coronado and his contemporaries sought only gold and silver. The prospectors who came later were little different in their quest, yet to many the search was more important than the strike.

They were a hardy band, those early prospectors who poked and plodded through ranges bearing names as diverse as Superstition and Old Dad, Sheep Hole and Rand, Bullion and Big Maria. Sometimes they found riches, more often not. Most of them died there. Some disappeared into the hills and were never seen again, while the final resting place of others was a heap of stones piled high to discourage foraging varmints.

The desert breeds fables, mysteries, tales of vast, hidden rewards awaiting only a prospector's pick—a hillside covered with nuggets, a rich mine of some long-gone prospector, its portal hidden beneath boulders washed upon it by some huge cloudburst. Mary Austin, who lived on the edge of those days, once wrote that it might be better to be bitten by the irascible sidewinder of the desert than by the tale of a lost mine.

Many of those who wandered into the desert between the California gold rush and the end of the century were on the run from what little law and justice there was in the West. An uncounted number were killed by Indians who looked upon lone white men as fair game—interlopers upon their land. A writer of that time pointed out that there was little mourning their departure; most of them needed killing. The desert and its canyons have long been a haven for the desperate and the damned. Horse thieves, murderers, miscreants of every kind have called the desert home. Within recent memory one Manson sent his "family" of followers out of the Panamints to descend upon Los Angeles to kill, mutilate, and dismember.

But Time, given a chance, is a civilizer. Outlaws and fugitives were outnumbered by moderately respectable men who followed their burros throughout the length and breadth of the American desert in search of gold and silver. Probably those who prospected in the hidden valley among the ranges that edge the northern Mojave were tougher than most. The first white men to stumble into it left part of their number stretched dead there upon the stony ground. For years, the trail of their passage through was marked by the bones of men and oxen, and the dried, split, iron-bound skeletons of wagons they abandoned here.

When these first strangers finally made their way out, they turned about and cursed it and gave it a name that has persisted for more than a hundred years—Death Valley. The Shoshone of this bleak land called it *Tomesha*—Ground Afire. Both names are awesomely apt.

Somewhere at a point not exactly known lies the bottom of the continent, a depression that lies almost three hundred feet below sea level. Here, in the desolate heart of the desert, nothing lives—no plant, no animal, no fish, no bird. Indeed, should any falter in this place of pure salt, it would be chemically embalmed. A thermometer in the center of this flat (should there happen to be one handy and anyone nearby to observe it) would probably climb higher than anywhere on earth.

Yet there are those who have come to terms with it, who have lived near the heart of the valley, if not at ease, at least in tolerable comfort. The Shoshone have lived here since time immemorial, leaving it only in hottest summer to climb the canyons of the Panamints to upper slopes, gathering piñon nuts and berries on the cooler ridges. Remnants of their descendants still live here on the mesquite flats south of Furnace Creek.

Close upon the heels of the first whites to pass this way was the family Lee—five brothers whose whimsical father must have had a knowledge of ancient Greek for he named his sons Alexander, Leander, Philander, Meander, and Salamander. They married Paiute and Shoshone squaws, so it is said, but the doubt is overwhelming that these liaisons were ever blessed by a ceremony of any kind. The practice of assigning unusual names remained a tradition in those bestowed upon the third generation of Lees. A half-breed son of one of the brothers was casually christened One Sock Lee, the only name he ever had. A daughter was called Peanuts Lee, while upon three other offspring were bestowed even more startling names—four-letter words found written only upon walls or in modern novels. But the Lees proved that white men could live in Death Valley in spite of all obstacles.

There was a continual passage of prospectors. They hunted silver and gold; they found both and by accident discovered rich deposits of borax. Word of such strikes drew lean and hungry men from all over the West. Roaring mining camps sprang up where the biggest strikes were made. Some were permanent and became towns that still remain; others crumbled back into the ground when the prospectors and miners departed for newer strikes of greater promise. Probably none had a more rapid rise and fall than Panamint City, nine thousand feet high in Surprise Canyon, over the crest of the range from Death Valley.

Panamint City came into being in April 1873, when the first silver was found. It rose out of nothing and flourished; at one time as many as 2,500 souls were claimed proudly in an article within the pages of the journal of that time and place, the *Panamint News*. But before long, the expense of extracting the silver from the complex metallurgical combinations in which it was locked grew beyond the capabilities of the mill there and the financial willingness of its owners. By May 1877, Panamint City was moribund—its mines standing unworked, its tents, stores, and saloons abandoned or gone. Only a handful of die-hard optimists remained. They hung on until an enormous cloudburst sent millions of tons of water and debris coursing down the canyon and wiped out its only road. The optimists gave up and departed.

All that remains of Bagdad is the old railway station, where no passengers wait and no trains stop.

Yet the history of hidden riches in the desert has always been one of optimism. Men who followed their burros up every steep canyon looking for gold and silver were optimists of the highest order. They had to be—more often than not, they found little of what they sought. When they did, they staked their claims, took out enough ore to make a showing, and headed for the nearest mining camp to shout the glad tidings. They seldom worked their claims; even if they had wanted to, that took more money than they had. They became not miners with a gold mine, but prospectors with a claim for sale. Wilier men, who knew with whom they dealt, bought claims for a fraction of their worth. The prospectors set up the drinks until the money ran out, begged another grubstake, and set off again following their burros toward the distant, blue mountains.

Avaricious they were not; gold was merely a means to an end, a way to meagerly finance a life as free as any our civilization has known. The quest was paramount; the attained goal almost anticlimax. Few of them could handle success or even momentary affluence. The great mining fortunes of the West seldom bore the names of lowly prospectors; they bore the names of those who were quick to exploit what these seekers found.

They were a picturesque bunch, these grizzled men who prowled the mountains bordering Death Valley early in this century. There was John LeMoigne, who had a yearning to spend his declining years taking his ease at the sidewalk cafes in Paris. He staked his claim soon after he came to Death Valley and sat on it for forty years, taking out enough to live on while he waited for a buyer who would pay him enough to return in style to his native France.

At length a group of mining engineers came, looked over his claim, and offered him eighty thousand dollars for it, proffering a sight draft on a San Francisco bank in payment. Old John refused. He wanted money, and these men offered him paper instead. John had been a country boy all his life; more than likely he had never been inside a bank. To John LeMoigne, money was golden and heavy, or green and official-looking; a piece of paper with writing was no substitute.

He never made it to France. He was still waiting for a buyer with real money when, in the summer of 1918, the blazing sun struck him down on the trail to Furnace Creek Ranch.

These adventurers left memorials behind them in the place-names marking the maps of the region. There was Darwin French, probably the first prospector to search in these hills—the village of Darwin in the foothills of the Argus Range is still a quiescent mining town patiently awaiting the next boom; Jack Salisbury gave his name unknowingly to the pass that climbs over the south flank of the Black Mountains between Shoshone and Death Valley. There was Jack Keane who left behind a ghost town to mark the site of Keane Wonder Mine, and Bill Ryan whose name is on the town that sits astride the borax deposits high above Furnace Creek Wash. In the north end of the valley stands that medieval monument to the most audacious fraud that ever set foot in the deserts of the American West—Walter Scott, forever enshrined in history as Death Valley Scotty.

But the man who left more of a mark than any other was Shorty Harris. Hardly taller than the smallest of his burros, Shorty prospected all around the edges of Death Valley. In his time, he was said to be responsible for five strikes of major proportions. Others said he never found anything, that he took credit for what others discovered, and proclaimed it so vociferously that his word prevailed. No matter—the truth is often divisible by two.

He found gold, but none of it ever stuck to his fingers. After he and Ed Cross discovered the Bullfrog in the Amargosa beyond the Grapevine Mountains, Shorty sold his share in the claim for nine hundred dollars and three barrels of whiskey—scarcely a better deal than the Indians negotiated when they sold Manhattan to Peter Minuit for twenty-four dollars and some glass trinkets. Shorty's money disappeared at the same rate as the whiskey. At the end of three weeks, Shorty was penniless again, and he was off following his burros across Death Valley, heading for the Panamints.

He met Pete Aguereberry along the trail, and high in the hills above Emigrant Wash, they made another strike at what came to be known first as Harrisberry and then Harrisburg. This time Shorty was wiser than before. He sold out for forty-two thousand shares in a company formed to exploit his claim. The first action of the new company was to assess each shareholder at the rate of two cents a share; Shorty's assessment was eight hundred forty dollars. Shorty had no money at all; they froze him out.

Vague and uncertain history claims that Shorty made other strikes—the St. Patrick that played out too soon, the World Beater that was too hard for one man to work. He had a rich mine near Gold Belt in the northern Panamints, but while he was away for supplies, someone stole the timbers, and the whole roof caved in.

So it went with Shorty—he was broke far more often than he was flush. Probably the greatest store of permanent wealth he ever possessed was when he traveled once to Los Angeles after making a modest strike and had all his teeth gold-plated. Thereafter his smile rivaled the golden sun of the desert.

He was part of the land—probably no white man before or since has been more completely one with this harsh environment. He cursed it, and

he loved it; he never left it. When he died some forty years ago, they buried him not far from the deepest depths of Death Valley and marked his grave with the epitaph: *Here lies Shorty Harris, single blanket jackass prospector.*

There were other men, now forgotten, who roamed this corner of the desert; other towns astride seams of gold or silver or borax that rose, flourished, and died. And with them went all the colorful characters who called Death Valley and its mountain environs home. They all are gone—the Indians Hungry Bill and Ann Cowboy, Indian George and Copperstain Joe, Mary Shoofly and Panamint Tom; the Lees, with their improbable names; Aaron Winters, who discovered borax, and F. M. Smith, who grew rich on it; the prospectors who searched every inch of the desert looking for bonanza, Dobe Charley and Sir Harry Oakes, Jacob Breyfogle and old Pete Harmon; Shorty Harris, that fine old man whose friends came from all over the American Southwest when they laid him to rest in the bottom of the desert. Their names are legion.

Probably the last to go was one August Ferge whose origins are murky, to say the least; he was loath to speak of his past. If his word could be believed, he skipped out from home somewhere in the East and worked his way westward odd-jobbing until he landed in Tonopah at the height of the gold fever there. He never left the goldfields. He made the rush to the Grandpa strike at Goldfield, on to the Bullfrog at Rhyolite; he was at Skidoo and Harrisburg, and ended up at Ballarat in 1912.

Ballarat lies at the base of the western slope of the Panamints where the road from Wildrose

drops down into the southern end of Panamint Valley. Nowadays, it doesn't look like much; there are one or two weathered wooden buildings, a handful of broken-down house trailers, skeletons of a few adobes melting back into the ground, piles of rusting junk—tin cans, old wire cables, wrecked Fords and Chevies and Dodges. In its heyday, between 1907 and 1917, it was lively enough. It was a supply and entertainment center for the claims in Pleasant Valley in the Panamints and those of the Argus Range across the valley.

There was a general store for grub and levis and dynamite and all the other necessities for those who came to extract ore from the ledges in the hills above. There were saloons aplenty to supply surcease and solace from a hard life. There were other establishments with music and painted ladies who offered sympathy and more in return for hard cash. But it ended the same as all the others. The claims played out, and there were no more found to replace them.

Some hold that the rise of Henry Ford was responsible for the decline of the goldfields. After the war of 1914–1918, prospectors in those parts turned their burros loose and took to driving Model T's as they went about the business of seeking their fortunes. It was not long after this that gold prospecting fell on thin days indeed. There were a thousand reasons given; those who were wisest knew the real reason why. When all the great strikes were made in the half-century following the boom in Panamint City, they were made by prospectors climbing the canyons in the hillsides looking for strayed burros. As they walked along, they looked, as prospectors will, at every ledge and outcropping, for traces of gold and silver; they found them. When they took to automobiles, all they looked for were nails in the road and potholes; they found them, too, but little else.

At any rate, Ferge came to Ballarat in its prime and stayed for sixty years through its decline and demise. He hung on so tenaciously that he *became* Ballarat, or what was left of it. He lived in a wooden shack and worked a few minor claims up above Post Office Springs; he took out enough to keep himself going, but not much more. Some who have other standards might have considered his life misspent; it never so entered Ferge's mind. He was a free man, and he was where he wanted to be, doing what he wanted to do. Few men can say as much.

As the years went by, all his old pals and sidekicks in the Death Valley country went on. The last to go was Shorty Harris, who died in 1934. Ferge didn't think much of the new people who came to the desert. He made himself scarce to newcomers. It followed naturally that this gaunt, unshaven man should come to represent Death Valley to newer generations. They called him Seldom Seen Slim, and he became known far beyond his own precincts. He was interviewed by a reporter from the *Los Angeles Times* and another from the *Christian Science Monitor*. People began to turn out of their way to see the last remaining desert rat.

He kept up his truculent façade, but underneath he enjoyed *being* somebody. Some city fellers, who came often, brought a bottle, and kept quiet while Slim told tall stories, were admitted to his restricted circle of friendship.

Some of these friends came to visit him one day in Ballarat and found him wasted away and near death of a malignancy. They carried him away to Trona. They put him in a clean, white bed in the hospital there; it was probably the best bed that Slim had ever occupied. It came too late to be enjoyed; Slim died the next day.

When they held his funeral a few days later at Ballarat, the old town recovered its excitement for a day. People came from Baker and Shoshone,

In the hot desert wind paint peels, wood weathers, and blowing sand etches away at both.

from Lone Pine and Mojave, from Trona and even Los Angeles. It was a warm summer day. They laid him in his coffin and set it in front of the crumbling abode that sits beside the road. Families with their children lined up beside the coffin to be photographed. There were young ladies in shorts and little else. There was cold beer by the case.

Slim would have enjoyed his own funeral. There was excitement; there were tall stories. All his friends were there, and six cronies—one had come all the way from Oregon to say goodbye—carried him to the graveyard. They planted him there; the preacher said a few words to celebrate this rite of passage. Everyone went back to town to drink the rest of the cold beer. There was much noise and gaiety before the old town grew empty at dark. Few men ever got such a pleasant send-off.

Now new generations roam these flats and hills. They come from cities in air-conditioned trailers, mobile homes, four-wheel-drive jeeps. They pass through in a hurry, or they make quick forays into the hills, looking for things of value. Then they go back to where they came from. At best they are momentary invaders or interlopers—*in* the desert, but not *of* it—at worst they are scavengers or vandals. Shorty Harris and his friends would have looked at them with contempt.

Gold and silver no longer come from these hills around Death Valley. It is still there, but there is no concerted action to remove it. No claims are bought and sold, no fortunes made. The nearest thing to a bonanza in the last fifty years occurred when an actor of less than stellar talent parlayed a television series about this des-

ert into a million dollars, a governorship, and presidential aspirations.

Gold and silver, copper and lead, borates and valuable deposits of all kinds are here awaiting another boom. When it comes, this desert will be destroyed to get at them.

On the steep slopes high above Emigrant Wash lies what is left of Skidoo, a gold town that flourished in the first decade of the century. As mining towns went in those days, it was advanced indeed. It had a telephone line that ran all the way to Rhyolite, and it had water piped in from permanent sources miles away on the slopes of Telescope Peak. Its name sprang from the popular jargon of the day, and it had its share of bravos and hell-raisers and drunks who followed the fortunes of the gold camps.

One of the more worthless was Joe Simpson, a part-time saloonkeeper who sampled too often and too well—so well, in fact, that locally he was known as "Hooch" Simpson. His particular wont was to take aboard an excess of spirits, take his six-shooter in hand, and stumble forth upon the single, stony street of Skidoo to seek someone to bedevil. The wonder is that someone had not done him in long before—if for nothing else, simply because he was a traffic hazard.

One fine Sunday morning he awoke after a brief respite from an all-night bout. Still drunk, he took a huge belt from the nearest bottle, seized his gun, and went forth to defy the world. Now in those days a gun-waving drunk staggering down the street of a mining town was not of sufficient novelty to cause undue excitement. More solid citizens simply walked in the other direction, women and children went indoors, stray dogs hid.

So it was, this day in Skidoo. No one took untoward notice of Hooch Simpson other than to exercise due caution in going about his business. But then Hooch took it into his head to crash into the Skidoo Mercantile Company, which was both bank and store. Clinging tightly to the counter to hold himself upright, he brandished his gun and announced thickly that he was holding up the bank.

In those hardier times, a robber barely able to stand was not taken too seriously. Several customers easily overpowered Hooch and relieved him of his gun. His partner was summoned from the Gold Seal Saloon across the street to take Hooch in hand, but to no avail. Hooch became more difficult and abusive by the minute. At length, the long-suffering store manager, one Jim Arnold, grabbed Simpson by the scruff of his neck and the seat of his pants, and threw him bodily out the door, across the plank porch, and into the rocky street. Hooch's partner herded him across to the Gold Seal and into the back room to sleep it off. A modicum of quiet returned to Skidoo.

But the saga of Hooch Simpson had not yet reached its climax. In the late afternoon Hooch awoke and began to brood on the fuzzily remembered humiliation he had suffered at the hands of the storekeeper. He took a stiff one to clear his head, and another, and yet another. The more he drank, the more monstrous became the affront to his dignity. By the time the bottle was half gone, Hooch had reached the same plateau he had occupied at the start of the morning's misadventures, and with this resurgence of bellicosity came an addled plan of action.

He searched the depths of the potbellied stove, where his partner usually hid Hooch's gun when he was unfit to possess it. It was there in the cold ashes. He took another stiff one and went out the back door and around to the front of the saloon. Reeling across the street, he stumbled into the Skidoo Mercantile Company, which was both bank and store.

Jim Arnold was there alone, so there was a scarcity of witnesses to recount exactly what happened. At any rate, less than a minute after Hooch entered the premises, Jim Arnold lay on the floor with a grievous hole in his mid-region while Hooch stumbled about.

At the sound of the shot, men poured in from a half-dozen nearby bars. They tried to lay hands upon Hooch, but since most of them were fully as drunk as he, the attempt was something less than efficient. There was a great deal of reeling around, shouting, and cursing, during which Hooch managed to squeeze off three rounds from his six-shooter. In the general confusion, someone—perhaps the lawman who had arrived, perhaps some other citizen strategically placed—managed to lay the butt of a Colt briskly across Hooch's skull, and he dropped like a stunned steer in a slaughterhouse. Before he could recover, he was dis-armed, carried down the street to a competitor's saloon, and tied to a chair, Skidoo being without a more fitting place of restraint.

Most of the town's hard-drinking males assembled at the same bar, and there was much drinking and recalling fond memories of popular Jim Arnold and casting imprecations upon the head of the sullen drunk tied up in the corner. The guzzling went on into the evening and late into the night.

In the middle of it, someone brought news of the demise of Jim Arnold. This called for many more rounds to the memory of stalwart Jim and curses upon the s.o.b. in the corner. As is often the case when tragedy strikes, those whom it brushes only lightly seize upon it as an excuse for a sort of dolorous celebration. So it was on this occasion, compounded by the fact that not only was Jim Arnold gone, but his departure marked the first murder Skidoo had ever had.

Whatever were the exact words and thoughts of the attendees at this wake will never be discovered. No one among them was sober enough to remember anything that occurred, and history was left only a vague and garbled account of it. But at some point, talk along the bar turned to justice and retribution.

Now in those times and in those purlieus, murder was most often charged up to self-defense, so that the more serious business of searching for gold would not be hampered by the inconvenience of trials, lawyers' con-

niving, and such. But the murder of good old Jim Arnold had been at the hands of a most unpopular cur, and the outrage of the populace was rabid indeed.

Sometime between midnight and dawn, the drunken assemblage along the bar passed judgment upon Hooch Simpson—a collective thumbs down. A stout rope was produced, and Hooch was led forth and hanged from the crossarm of a pole on the telephone line from Skidoo to Rhyolite. After his body had stopped jerking in the lantern light, the crowd surged back to the bar to lift another glass to the triumph of justice.

When the sun arose on Skidoo Monday morning and revealed the already stiffened body of Hooch Simpson slowly turning in the breeze, nobody seemed to know much about it. Those of his executioners who were still on their feet were hard at it along the bar of the Club Saloon. The rest of the citizens took one look at who was dangling there and decided it was a case of good riddance.

Later in the morning they cut his body down and unceremoniously laid him away. His partner was his only mourner, and even his grief was mingled with relief at this dissolution of a bothersome relationship.

In ordinary circumstances, the tale of Hooch Simpson would end here. But Skidoo was no ordinary place. It wasn't long before word of the happening reached the Owens Valley and even far-off Los Angeles. In a couple of days a reporter and photographer appeared to give full and appropriate coverage to the only lynching that ever occurred in any of the Death Valley diggings.

They were surprised to find no body hanging. Being enterprising newsmen in the best tradition of their profession, they set out to win the friendship of those in Skidoo whose friendship could be bought by liberal applications of whiskey. No one has left an accounting of how many rounds were set up on the bar of the Club Saloon before the exhilarants there succumbed to the reporter's blandishments, dug up Hooch's body, and strung him up again so the photographer could set up his camera and record the signal event.

Throughout the desert there are monuments that mark man's passage. The cave paintings in Ventana Cave may go back 110 centuries—as old a marking as humans have made in the New World. Mounds are all that remain of towns and villages of the prehistoric Hohokam; their counterparts are the ghost towns left behind by white men who came to take gold and silver from the hills and then moved on when the claims played out. Some of these towns date back to the time the first white men came from beyond the Mississippi to seek riches beneath the earth; others have been built and abandoned so recently that the lumber they were made of has yet to show the weathering marks of passing years.

Most of them were clusters of shacks and shanties that sprang up around more solid structures that housed the institutions of importance—the banks, saloons, bordellos, and assay offices. Some even had churches and schools, but most had no time for such things. Indeed, the majority rose, flourished, and were abandoned before such civilizing influences could ever be brought to bear.

Some of them were built more than once—fire spread easily in such dry timbers as these towns were made of. Other towns were built of stone and these have lasted longer, but vandals are doing a better job of ruination than the climate ever could. Some have disappeared almost completely—Amos and Harrisburg and Goldroad have been gone so long, there is little left to mark their existence except scattered relics and vanishing memories. Others—Amboy and Essex and Bagdad—lasted longer, but new highways across the desert have passed them by and removed their season for being. Talc City is so newly empty that it has barely begun to disintegrate. Calico has been siezed upon by enterprising men and turned into a working ghost town to attract tourists; in that role it may last forever.

The great highways across the desert are seldom quiet; both day and night find them pulsing with life.

There are other towns poised in limbo awaiting either renewal or oblivion—saved for the moment from becoming ghost towns because the mines that brought them into being still hold gold and silver; their owners await a change in the monetary policy of the nation, a change that may make them all rich again. Until then Darwin and Vidal, Johannesburg and Keeler, Quartzsite and Oatman and Randsburg and a dozen others drowse in the desert sun waiting. They share their memories with the elderly retired who have begun to settle in them. These wait, too, but not for gold; mostly they wait in the sun for time to catch up with them.

There are other monuments that man has built and left behind to mark his passage. Roads the Indians and Spaniards and Mexicans made in the centuries before the present one are only faint traces in the desert. It was left to modern man to limit their aimlessness and increase their utility. He eventually paved them so that in all times and all seasons the flow of men and machines— more across the desert than within—would not be slowed.

As with most marks of man here, these highroads are eminently visible; they stretch like long ribbons as far as the eye can see, black double stripes against sandy desert soil. At night, along these freeways, headlamps of cars and huge trucks make a pageant of light sometimes visible

Retirees, flocking to the Mojave in search of warmth and peace, have erected signs to mark their presence.

times past were major highways that now only occasionally hear the sound of passing traffic. Some back roads have names that are quite obvious—Sidewinder Road, Butterfield Stage Road—while others are named for events that have faded beyond memory—Old Woman Road, Sorefinger Road. There is one in the middle of the Mojave with that most improbable of names—Zzxyzx Road. What it commemorates is a nagging mystery.

Some have no names at all and are at best highways to nowhere, petering out in aimless tracks that disappear into creosote bush flatlands or impassable washes. Some lead to towns that once were lively with the commerce of gold and silver and the sound of rushing traffic. Now they are roads to nowhere, too.

across scores of miles as far as vision persists. They look like mainstreets in the desert which is precisely what they are, efficiently designed to move great numbers of vehicles across the desert as quickly as possible to Los Angeles, to Bakersfield, to Flagstaff, Phoenix, Tucson, and beyond. The busiest of them all, that great artery of anticipation or regret, depending upon direction of travel, leads three hundred miles across the Mojave between Los Angeles and Las Vegas. The travelers on this highway likely never see the desert, except as an ordeal to be put behind as quickly as possible.

Roads turn off the freeways to wander in the desert. Sometimes they lead nowhere; others in

There is a compelling attraction in certain of the monuments that man has left behind him in the desert to commemorate the final resting places of his brothers. The Anglo-Saxons term them cemeteries, but Mexicans give them better names—*campos santos*, or "holy fields."

These forlorn and often forgotten plots, their crosses and headstones askew, are one with the desert. Unlike proper city cemeteries with green lawns and rank after rank of well-kept marble monuments, desert graves have a tumbledown, abandoned look—simply another of man's remnants discarded in these scorched lands.

Most of the grave markers are wooden, with names roughly carved or crudely painted upon them. Now and then there is a more pretentious marble headstone, carved with bands of tiny angels frozen triumphant or with the clasped hands of friendship not often encountered in those early days. It leans at an awkward angle or lies flat upon the ground. The wooden markers never rot away as in damper climates; instead they fall victim to an enemy just as persistent and relentless—the constant abrasion of fine, wind-blown sand that etches at the grain of the wood and soon renders nameless those the markers celebrate. Even the custom of turning them away from prevailing winds proved useless; sharp sand still wore them away. Nor could harder stone withstand the winds; over the years incised names were sanded away and made indecipherable.

The mounds above the graves have long since disappeared, sunken now so that crosses keep a vigil over depressions that indicate the dimensions of those that lie beneath. The frequency of small depressions mutely demonstrates the high mortality rate among infants in those early times.

Where stone slabs were laid, small rodents have carved out caves and tunnels to hide from heat and a congregation of voracious enemies—hawks and coyotes and snakes. Sometimes a creosote bush or tornadillo stands above a grave, higher than other plants in the nearby desert, signaling the discovery of some unusual resource at its roots. Where mourners still remain to recall the past existence of those who lie here, they

Older markers, toppling in neglected graveyards, are all that remain of some earlier desert settlements.

decorate the graves with small clusters of imitation flowers, which never fade or die but sit there in glass jars, keeping plastic vigil among the brown and sere grasses.

Whether by accident or design, these rude western graveyards seem always to be located on the slopes of some bajada overlooking cluttered signs of human habitation below. Probably the survivors earnestly hoped that the departed had left this life to journey to some higher place, and so had planted them on some earthly eminence to signify this new and loftier state. On the other hand, it may have been to get them out of the way of more prosperous locations nearby where lay gold and silver and all the other precious things they sought.

As he did throughout the length and breadth of the western hemisphere, the white man brought his European traditions with him and imposed them on all the subjugated peoples he overcame. So it is that the original inhabitants of the desert abandoned whatever burial rites and customs they had and gathered their dead together in ordered plots with all the trappings of the Roman Church. But since the white man forbade them to wander beyond certain carefully defined limits, they have not moved on and abandoned the resting places of their ancestors. While the graveyards of the white man for the most part slowly disintegrate and crumble back into the desert untended and unnoticed, the campo santo of the Indian does so to a far lesser degree. On holy days of the dead, the graves are bright with

the brilliance of plastic flowers. New flowers are added with each new occasion of celebration, and the graves are never without color. These cemeteries of the Indians always have a comparatively cheerful look about them, usually the only bright spot of color to last the year round in the entire sweep of the desert.

There are touches that smack of Mexico among the Papago who live along the border between Arizona and Sonora. Along highways where Papago, like most other Indians not really at home behind the wheel of alien automobiles, have met their deaths in the grinding crash of cars meeting head-on at high speeds, are small shrines—white crosses, with the ubiquitous plastic flowers and often a brightly burning candle, sheltered from the wind and tended carefully by some stoic widow or mother.

But through them all—through the holy places of Papago and Pima and Paiute, the cemeteries of Ballarat and Bullfrog and Bagdad—blows the restless, probing desert wind carrying the fine sand that relentlessly carves away at the sole tangible memory of those who passed this way and fell and stayed behind to become a part of the desert.

In time they will all disappear—gravestones, backroads, and deserted towns. Blowing sands may sculpture them to extinction or cover them with drifts; cloudbursts may bring down clay and stone from the mountains to bury them. But more than likely vandal man will get there first and leave little for wind and water to do.

death valley

OVERLEAF: *Walls of canyons descending*
from the Panamints are scoured by plunging floodwaters
loaded with sand, pebbles, and boulders . . .

. . . while salts leached from many mountains
spread out white upon the barren playas—alkali flats
that mark the bottom of the continent.

High dunes of sand as fine and white as sugar move restlessly
before the wind, and the river that wanders slowly into the valley
is hardly more than an artery of salt.

*Borax deposits, cut and furrowed by erosion, support no life,
but beneath the sand dunes lie hidden stores of moisture that invite
desert plants to send down roots to drink.*

*In time's slow drama the mud hills yield to the steady onslaught of the elements,
and their strata of umber, red, and gray melt gradually back into the desert.*

*On the long Baja peninsula there grows a wild jungle of cardon, boojum,
and cholla—a succulent forest of incredible proportions.*

Old roads meander through boojums and lichen-encrusted rocks
in an unhurried passage to the blue mountains beyond.

OVERLEAF: *In dry months, before gathering storms
bring moisture to replenish the parched earth, tall ocotillo
stand bare and gaunt against the hot sunrise sky.*

139

Bark peels continuously from the elephant tree, leaving its trunk bare and bulbous,
clothed only in a lacework of scattered limbs and leaflets.

Epilogue

THE CASE FOR DESERT

Whenever opportunity presents itself, I seize upon the chance to head for the desert. If time is short, the Mojave suffices; wandering among sand dunes at Kelso or Shoshone or climbing the Providence Mountains to look for bighorn sheep is surcease enough from tension and pressure. If time is longer, then the park at Organpipe or the higher reaches of the Huachucas in Arizona beckon. Occasionally I find myself deep in Sonora or far down the long peninsula of Baja California. But it matters not which desert—the first sight of Joshua tree or saguaro or boojum is as much an exhilaration as it was when I first began to travel here fifteen years ago.

Sometimes my path leads to a small, century-old town between Phoenix and Tucson where my sister comes to spend the cooler months on the edge of the desert, seeking escape from the torments of arthritis. It is a comfortable house that stands alone; there are no other houses within a quarter-mile. The grounds are a delight of saguaro, prickly pear, and desert trees.

Often my brother-in-law and I drive across the desert, through Pima lands, past ancient Hohokam mounds that hide their abandoned villages. We talk about the desert, and he, a most pragmatic and anthropocentric man, looks out upon the immense stretch of creosote bush and cactus and arid mountains and asks, as he has done before, "But what is it good for?"

The question comes back to bother me when we return to the pleasant house on the edge of the teeming, arid garden that is the desert. There is nothing that frets me more than to have no answer to reinforce my point of view. So I think upon it while sitting beside the picture window that overlooks the small desert garden of cholla, prickly pear, and palo verde.

Beyond, along the banks of the dry wash, there are luxuriant creosote bushes higher than a man's head and saguaro thirty or more feet tall. My sister hangs great lumps of suet in the palo verde tree and spreads handfuls of wild bird seed upon the ground. We spend much time watching the pageant of life that parades through the garden—this patch that is the desert in microcosm.

There are always brassy cactus wrens and curve-billed thrashers at the seeds and in the water bath. Red cardinals make a brilliant streak of color as they wing in to nibble at a seed or two before flying to the highest branch of the palo verde to send a torrent of melody upon the day.

Bands of plump Gambrel's quail hop along the low rock wall, tense at any sign of danger. The male has a piercing cry of warning that he sometimes voices. Some say he cries *"Chi-ca-go,"* but this is patently ridiculous; he has never been near the place. This fat bird lives in a land where Spanish has been a native tongue for more than four centuries; he cries out *"Cui-da-do"* when he senses danger, which any small *paisano* will tell you means "Take care!" in Spanish. Satisfied that all is well, the covey hops down to mingle with white-winged doves from Mexico and Inca doves scarcely larger than sparrows.

Gilded flickers and gila woodpeckers nest in saguaro at the edge of the garden. They are wary, coming infrequently to drink or to peck at the suet. Sometimes a roadrunner hops along the wall to see if anything here is worth his notice. He disdains the offered food but condescends to drink our water.

Most of the birds of the desert have paused within this garden—yellow-headed verdins, lark buntings, and red-eyed cowbirds; finches and glossy black phainopeplas; towhees that scratch like chickens for seed hidden in the grass. Orioles are here in spring, and elf owls come at twilight to search for prey.

Small Yuma antelope squirrels live in dozens of holes in the banks of the wash. With white tails held high, they come out into the garden to eat; they stay to play, to fight, and make love. Timid desert cottontails are always about, and an occasional black-tailed jackrabbit. Sometimes at first or last light, terrified birds and small animals flee for cover just as the pair of coyotes that live somewhere beyond the wash trot through to lap at the water dish and gaze with hunger at the suet hanging beyond their reach. Once a bobcat loped along the wall, a freshly-caught cottontail limp in his jaws. That same evening a mother skunk led her new family slowly through the garden before passing into a thicket of mesquite.

There have been other creatures here, unseen and unexpected. Once a spate of javelina footprints marked the sands of the wash after an evening's rainstorm. One night, long beyond midnight, the quiet was broken by cries of mortal terror that rent the blackness and then were suddenly stilled. Next morning we found shreds of fur and gouts of blood on the top of the rock wall; we never discovered what small thing met his end here or the agent of his death.

Once at dawn we saw beneath a prickly pear a serpent with diamond markings upon his back. The air was crisp this early spring morning, and he was too torpid to shake his rattles at our approach. His middle was swollen with the rabbit or squirrel he had eaten but not yet digested.

Beyond this desert garden lies the larger garden of the whole Sonoran Desert, an arid paradise where live millions of birds and animals and curious plants that choose this land above all others to abide in. It is pleasant enough for them; they flourish here. Where men have often found it too forbidding, these other living things have come to terms with it.

As I bumbled about this desert, giving forth exclamations of wonder and feeling need of little more, I found the answer to the question; I learned what this desert crowded with birds and saguaros, boojums and serpents, kangaroo rats and cholla is good for.

It's good for *them* and that is enough.

infinite vista

After a rain remnants of ancient lakes that lie scattered about
the northern Mojave again hold a few inches of water.

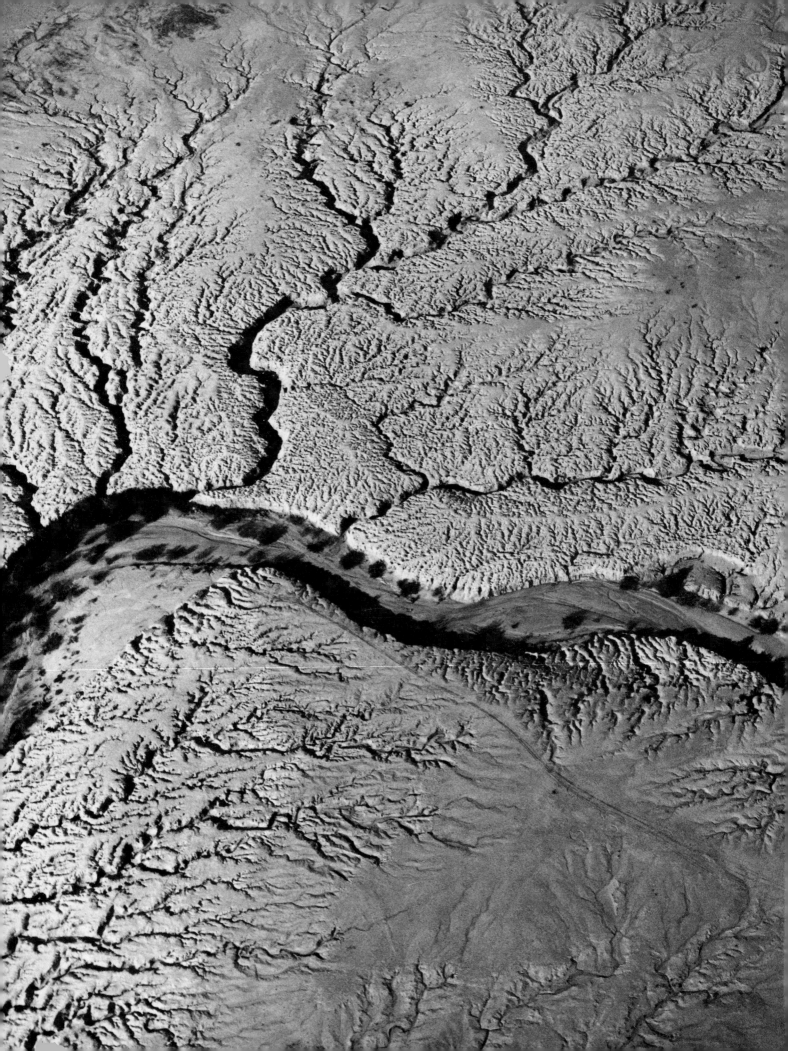

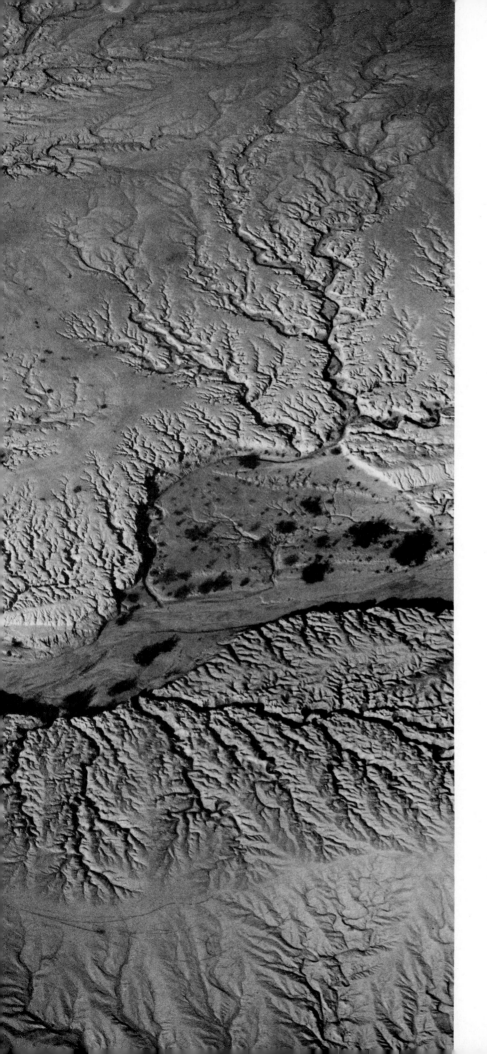

Where runoff from storms courses down the hillsides, it cuts converging channels, like a pattern of tree roots in reverse.

OVERLEAF: *Across the whole desert only one persistent stream, the Colorado, cuts it way to the sea.*

Roads crisscross the desert, some making their way
between the hills, others climbing across them.

OVERLEAF: *Through a thousand empty washes, long freight
trains crawl slowly along toward more populous lands.*

AFTERWORD

I first saw the desert almost half a century ago, when as an adolescent I traveled with my parents from Kansas City to Los Angeles to visit an older syster. We drove across the Mojave in a Dodge that cruised at thirty miles an hour. It was a daytime trip in mid-July—an experience that remains vivid in my memory to this day.

Earlier, when I was a small boy in my native Texas, a very old lady had told me how her father, my great-grandfather, had lost his life somewhere in the scorched lands of southern Arizona or northern Sonora while returning to Texas from the California gold fields. She never knew whether he had died of thirst or at the hand of some Indian or desperado who lay in wait for travelers with a full poke. She only knew that he had left Fort Yuma and was never heard of again.

I wondered about him as I crossed the desert that first time, and I felt sad that he had met his end in such a harsh and lonely place. Even today when I am in the southern desert, the thought often passes through my mind that this parched range of hills or that flat covered with creosote bush may hide my ancestor's final resting place. But as the years have gone by, my vision has grown wider. I have traveled often to this desert to linger when the sweet scent of palo verde blossoms fills the air and the song of the mockingbird is a midnight delight, and my love for it has grown apace. I am no longer sad about my great-grandfather's fate, for I am now convinced that there could be no finer place to spend an eternity than in this arid garden.

A personal project of any magnitude can scarcely be accomplished without help from someone else. This particular effort was helped frequently along its way. Probably the foremost assistance came from the dedicated research librarian at Carmel's Harrison Memorial Library, Anna Binicos, who made valuable suggestions and found source material that I did not know existed, from libraries scattered over several states. Hers was a major contribution.

Dr. Warren Thompson of the Naval Postgraduate School, Monterey, California, sat down more than once with me and patiently led me through the complexities of jet streams, high pressure areas, and other weather phenomena until I came to understand the causes for the desert's existence.

I am deeply indebted to Dr. Emil Haury, of the University of Arizona at Tucson, who took the time to talk to me about those desert people he knows better than anyone else does—the ancient Hohokam. It was he who so aptly described the desert Indian: "He rested lightly upon the land." This original phrase, coined during our conversations, fired my interest and led me upon journeys of discovery about these venerable inhabitants. Dr. Bernard Fontana, of the same university, was a generous source of information about water usage and water rights on the desert.

My thanks to Arnold Allison, of Sacaton on the Pima Reservation, for the time he took to escort me about his homeland, telling me old tales and showing me ancient ruins and holy places; to Joseph Karol of Florence, Arizona, who took me among the Papago people and introduced me to his friends there; to Father James Chin of Mission San Xavier del Bac and Father Lambert Fremdling of Mission San Jose at Pisinimo, who told me much about the ways of the Papago.

I am extremely grateful to Ted Shonk, who put himself and his Cessna at my disposal to crisscross the desert and see it in a new way; and to E. K. Balls for assistance with certain troubling botanical identifications. (If there are errors, they are mine alone.)

John Chakeres, Jim Hill, and Sjef Wildschut, fellow photographers, made excursions into the desert with me and were of great help in providing companionship and expertise.

I would like to thank four I have never met, authors who wrote with love for the American deserts: Joseph Wood Krutch, Peggy Larson, Ruth Kirk, and above all, Mary Austin. Their works are a treasure chest for any who would learn more of these lands.

To those others who have helped but whom I have overlooked, my deep thanks and gratitude. And finally to many nameless Mexicans who put up with my flawed Spanish and, with smiles, sped me on my way—*gracias*.

PHOTOGRAPHIC NOTES

The photographs on these pages were made with cameras of varied size and format. For most I used a single-lens reflex, the Mamiya RB67—a most versatile camera and my own particular workhorse—with four Sekor lenses, 50mm, 90mm, 250mm, and 360mm. A few photographs each were made with a Mamiyaflex C2, a Rolleiflex, a Hasselblad, and a 4x5 Calumet view camera. Most of the aerials and wildlife photographs were made with a Minolta SRT 101.

I use a tripod whenever possible. In addition to standard ones, I use a small tripod only six inches high with the 35mm and 120 cameras. This provides me with a new and different viewpoint that is often highly effective.

The black-and-white photographs were made using Ilford's Pan F, FP4, and HP4; Kodak's Panatomic-X and Tri-X; GAF's Versapan; and Agfa's Agfapan 25. Film developers were HC-110, FG-7, and Rodinal. Ordinarily, I am a strong advocate of using only one slow, one medium, and one fast film. However, during the time of working on this book, old favorite films were discontinued and new ones introduced. Therefore, my film and developer combinations were tested in the field to find new materials that were satisfactory to me. (For the curious, my final choices are Pan F, FP4, and Tri-X in the roll films, and Versapan in the sheet film.) Ansel Adams' Zone System of exposure and development were followed. All prints were made on Ilfrobrome double weight glossy graded papers, developed in Amidol or Dektol.

Almost all of the color film used was Ektachrome Professional. When other films or a camera other than the Mamiya RB67 were used, it is so indicated in the photographic details which follow.

In only five or six cases are the photographs in this book cropped, and then only because of compositional demands in the book layout. More than one art director has complained that it is difficult to crop my photographs. I look upon this as a measure of success. The great photographer Ernst Haas has said that the ground glass of the camera is the photographer's discipline; within its limits he can include or exclude, and all things within it must work toward the reinforcement of the final image. To me, this is the essence of photography—the "seeing" that insures the success or failure of the final image.

Photographic Details

PAGES 2–3: Hedgehog cactus (*Echinocereus sp.*), Organpipe National Monument, Arizona. 50mm Sekor.

PAGES 4–5: High altitude desert (12,000 feet) in the White Mountains above the northern Mojave. White Mountain Peak in the distance is, at 14,242 feet, only slightly lower than Mount Whitney. 4x5 Calumet, 8″ Symmar.

PAGES 6–7: Beetle tracks on a Death Valley dune. 90mm Sekor.

PAGES 10–11: Saguaro (*Carnegiea gigantea*) on cliffs in the Santa Catalina range near Tucson. 250mm Sekor.

PAGE 12: Palm Canyon, Kofa Mountains, Arizona. In this range is a rich mine named "The King of Arizona." The mountains' name is an acronym of the mine's. 90mm Sekor.

PAGES 12–13: Backlit rocks, Alabama Hills, Owens Valley, California. 4x5 Calumet, 8″ Symmar, Agfachrome.

PAGES 14–15: Run-off from a flash flood in Death Valley. Minolta, 28mm Auto-Rokkor, Kodachrome 25.

PAGE 15: Cracked mud, Eureka Valley, California. 90mm Sekor.

PAGE 16: Yucca and rock, Joshua Tree National Monument, California. 90mm Sekor.

PAGE 19: Smoke tree (*Dalea spinosa*) in a Mojave wash near Essex, California. 90mm Sekor, Agfapan 25.

PAGE 20: Creosote bush (*Larrea divaricata*) and saguaro on the Papago Reservation, Arizona. 250mm Sekor, Agfapan 25.

PAGE 23: Storm clouds over the Avawatz Mountains north of Baker, California. 4x5 Calumet, 6½″ Wollensak Raptar, Versapan.

PAGE 27: Rock formations, Mojave. 90mm Sekor, Panatomic-X, orange filter.

PAGE 31: Lenticular clouds in the Eureka Valley, California. 90mm Sekor, Panatomic-X, red and polarizing filters.

PAGE 33: Joshua trees, Joshua Tree National Monument. Rolleiflex, 80mm Schneider Xenar, Panatomic-X.

PAGES 34–35: Saguaro and chainfruit cholla (*Opuntia fulgida*), Superstition Mountains, Arizona. 90mm Sekor, Agfapan 25, red filter.

PAGE 36: Clump of senita cactus (*Lophocereus schotti*), Organpipe National Monument. 90mm Sekor, FP4.

PAGE 37: Trunk of a giant saguaro, Kofa Mountains, Arizona. 250mm Sekor, Panatomic-X.

PAGE 38. TOP: Our Lord's candle (*Yucca whipplei*) in desert ranges, Baja California. 4x5 Calumet, 8″ Symmar, Versapan. BOTTOM: Senita cactus. 250 Sekor, Agfapan 25.

PAGES 38–39: Barrel cactus (*Ferocactus wislizenii*) and Spanish dagger (*Yucca mojavensis*), Providence Range, Mojave Desert. 50mm Sekor, Pan F.

PAGE 40: Leaves of the Joshua tree (*Yucca brevifolia*), Mojave Desert. 90mm Sekor, Pan F.

PAGE 49: Blossom of prickly pear cactus (*Opuntia santa-rita*), Saguaro National Monument, Arizona. 90mm Sekor.

PAGES 50–51: Cholla (*Opuntia bigelovii*) and desert hills, Oatman, Arizona. 90mm Sekor.

PAGE 52: Saguaro blossoms. 250mm Sekor.

PAGES 52–53: Saguaro in winter storm, Florence, Arizona. 90mm Sekor.

PAGE 54: Fruiting senita cactus, Sonoran Desert, Mexico. 250mm Sekor.

PAGE 55. TOP: Senita cactus, Baja California. 90mm Sekor. BOTTOM: Black-throated sparrow (*Amphispiza bilineata*) perched in cholla clump, Sonoran Desert, Mexico. Minolta, 1200mm MTO mirror optic, High Speed Ektachrome.

PAGE 56: Mound cactus (*Echinocereus mojavensis*), White Mountains, California. 90mm Sekor.

PAGE 57: Lizard on rock, Colorado River Canyon near Blythe, California. Minolta, 200mm Auto-Rokkor, High Speed Ektachrome.

PAGE 58. TOP: Detail of barrel cactus, Baja California. 90mm Sekor. BOTTOM: Barrel cactus and agave, Vizcaíno Desert, Baja California. 4x5 Calumet, 8″ Symmar.

PAGE 59: Blossoms of staghorn cholla (*Opuntia acanthocarpa*), Organpipe National Monument. 4x5 Calumet, 6½″ Wollensak Raptar, Agfachrome.

PAGE 60. TOP: Blossoms of beavertail cactus (*Opuntia basilaris*) along the Bill Williams River, Arizona. 90mm Sekor. BOTTOM: Desert tortoise (*Gopherus agassizi*), Chocolate Mountains, California. 90mm Sekor.

PAGE 61: Desert lily (*Hesperocallis undulata*) near Twenty-nine Palms, California. 90mm Sekor.

PAGES 62–63: Prince's plume (*Stanleya pinnata*), Owens Valley. 90mm Sekor.

PAGE 64: Astragalus, Joshua Tree National Monument. 90mm Sekor.

PAGES 64–65: Desert primrose (*Oenothera deltoides*) and desert senna (*Cassia armata*), Mojave Desert. 90mm Sekor.

PAGE 66. TOP: Yucca plants (*Y. arizonica*) near Nogales, Arizona. 90mm Sekor. BOTTOM: Yellow-headed blackbird (*Xanthocephalus xanthocephalus*) along lower Colorado River near Blythe. Minolta, 1200mm MTO mirror optic, High Speed Ektachrome.

PAGES 66–67: Palo verde (*Cercidium floridum*) and saguaro in desert wash, Eagletail Mountains, Arizona. 90mm Sekor.

PAGE 68. TOP: Butterfly on desert flowers near Sinaloa-Sonora border, Mexico. 250mm Sekor. BOTTOM: Locust on desert plant near Guaymas, Sonora. 250mm Sekor.

PAGE 69. TOP: Flowering fishhook cactus (*Mammillaria sp.*) near Carbo, Sonora. 90mm Sekor. BOTTOM: Pods on dried vine near Carbo. 90mm Sekor.

PAGES 70–71: Salt flat in Death Valley near Badwater. 90mm Sekor.

PAGE 71: Wild burros in the Panamint Range, Death Valley National Monument. 250mm Sekor.

PAGE 72: Yucca (*Y. valida*), Magdalena Desert, Baja California. 50mm Sekor.

PAGE 81: Road signs on the Papago Reservation, Arizona. Mamiyaflex C2, 180mm Sekor, Panatomic-X.

PAGE 82. TOP: Roadside shrine, Papago Reservation. 90mm Sekor, Agfapan 25, red filter. BOTTOM: Crosses along the road, marking the site of a major accident in which nine Indians were killed. 90mm Sekor, Panatomic-X.

PAGES 82–83: Ceremonial wine house, Papago Reservation. 50mm Sekor, Agfapan 25.

PAGE 84: Outbuilding made of adobe, straw, and ocotillo staves, Papago Reservation. 90mm Sekor, Agfapan 25.

PAGE 85: Margaret Saraficio, conceded to be among the finest, if not the finest, of the Papago basketmakers. 250mm Sekor, FP4.

PAGE 86: Benito Garcia, Papago medicine man. 250mm Sekor, FP4.

PAGE 87. TOP: Rosa Andrew, Papago Indian girl. 250mm Sekor, FP4. BOTTOM: Jose Flores, a Papago elder of more than ninety summers, San Xavier del Bac, Arizona. 250mm Sekor, Tri-X.

PAGE 88: Ernest and Dolores Andrew, Papago Indians. 250mm Sekor, FP4.

PAGE 89: Mission founded by Father Kino, Tumacacori National Monument, Arizona. 90mm Sekor.

PAGE 90: Mission Caborca, Sonora. This is another of Kino's missions. Twice it was the scene of massacres—once in the seventeenth century, when Indians killed the priests, and again almost two hundred years later, when a party of invading American freebooters were killed by Mexican militiamen shortly before our Civil War. 50mm Sekor.

PAGE 91: Interior of mission at Pisinimo, Papago Indian Reservation. Although Catholic ceremonies are performed, the decoration is Indian. 90mm Sekor.

INDEX

(Italic numbers indicate illustrations.)